WINNING HOME

An Organization for Children

WINNING HOME

An Organization for Children

Patricia J. Brady

Winning Home
125th Anniversary History
Winning Home, Inc., P.O. Box 1308, Concord, MA 01742
winninghome.org

ISBN: 979-8-218-39247-5

Printed in the United States of America

Cover photograph: Courtesy of the Winchester Archival Center

First Printing: April 2024

Dedication

To Thomas J. Martin III
(1940-2023)
For more than 50 years of service to
Winning Home
as a member of the Board of Directors,
including two terms as President.
His kindness, dedication and generosity
benefited generations of children.

Preface

It began as a 19th century farm that sprawled more than a hundred acres across the beautiful hills north of Boston where the communities of Woburn, Winchester and Lexington come together. After a century as a farm, it became a summer camp operated by a popular Boston minister, who brought children there from the city's South End when the South End was Boston's poorest neighborhood. A settlement house then took over the camp and placed additional emphasis on educating the children. Eventually the summer camp for children from the city became a local organization serving young people from the three suburban communities it overlapped. And then it became something completely different: a grant-maker supporting nonprofit organizations helping children in Woburn, Winchester, Lexington and a dozen nearby communities.

The organization is called Winning Home, and its history is told in the following pages. It's a heartwarming tale, full of city children visiting a genuine farm, encountering chickens and cows for the first time, taking rides in a hay-wagon, giving baths to baby lambs. It was a summer camp when summer camping was new, and kids were just starting to spend time in the countryside learning archery, engaging in arts and crafts, gathering around campfires at nightfall, and sleeping in tents or cabins.

But it's also a story about children living through hard times, kids who came to the farm never having seen a tree, or a sunset. These were the urchins in historic photographs, hollow-eyed children working long days in textile mills from the age of five or six. They came to the farm as to a refuge. Later came children of the Great Depression, when so many American families slipped into poverty, and later still, children of the period when urban poverty was spreading to the suburbs. Needy children were everywhere.

Winning Home has a tale to tell about a plain farmer and his desire to alleviate some of the suffering of his time. It is the story of an early 20th century New England charity fulfilling its mission to help children through changing times and unexpected challenges. The organization that emerged from the farmer's legacy provided life-long memories of summer camping for generations of children, and after nearly disappearing during hard times of its own, found new and different and more varied ways to help children in the present—and into the future.

Contents

William Henry Winning, Farmer:
A country childhood, a single life, a successful career, a remarkable will

When Woburn farmer William Henry Winning died in 1898, he left a large bequest for the care of orphans and destitute children. He himself had grown up on the thinly populated western edge of town where his family's sprawling farm occupied more than a hundred acres of classic New England countryside. There were wildflower meadows among tall trees, a peach orchard and an apple orchard, a meandering stream, a big barn, a number of cows grazing in quiet pastures, a lot of long slopes covered with blueberry bushes, and scattered patches of dense woods. It was a beautiful place to grow up, and, perhaps guessing that less fortunate children would enjoy it too, Winning left his farm for their benefit.

Well into the 20th century, children came to the farm from Boston's South End, then the city's poorest, most crowded, and least healthful neighborhood. They stayed for a week or two in the summer. They drank clean milk from the farm's herd of cows, consumed fresh food grown on the premises, explored the woods with counselors who pointed out insects and flowers, sang songs around a campfire as night came on, and slept in a bed of their own.

William Winning had no children himself. He was a market gardener who had done well. A newspaper obituary described him as "industrious,"[1] an admiring term and a necessary quality for a successful farmer then as always. But who was he, what was his life like, and how did he acquire the fortune he so generously bequeathed at his death?

Left: William Winning would have taken his wares to Boston's Quincy Market—the regional wholesale market that opened in 1826. Boston Public Library, Creative Commons license.

William Henry Winning was born in 1836, the youngest, along with a twin sister, of five children of John and Nancy Locke Winning. The elder Winning was a yeoman farmer—one who owned rather than rented his land—and thus enjoyed a degree of social status. He had come to Woburn from Billerica and on June 2, 1830, purchased a tract of land from the Wright family containing 134 acres more or less, with the dwelling house and barn and outbuildings thereon, for $2,650.[2] The land had most likely been cultivated by Native Americans of the Massachusett tribe and the Pawtucket people, and, after the European arrival, by the Wrights, who were among the founders and earliest settlers of Woburn. John Winning's acreage lay partly in Woburn, partly in present-day Winchester (which was part of Woburn until 1850), and partly in Lexington.

The farm, 1901. Courtesy, Winchester Archival Center

The spacious farm on which William Henry Winning would grow up constituted a world unto itself in that era, when farms were like independent fiefdoms, and farm families met all of their own needs. Men, and often women, plowed and planted and cultivated the land. Women spun and wove and sewed the family's clothing and made household items such as soap and candles. Children helped from an early age, acquiring career skills almost from the cradle. It is not surprising, perhaps, that "Self-Reliance," Ralph Waldo Emerson's classic essay celebrating individualism, appeared during this period of American history.

But change was in the air. The year before William Winning was born the railroad arrived in Woburn, and the nation's first regional canal, the Middlesex, had begun transporting the town's goods a bit earlier. Woburn was becoming a microcosm of the new nation, a dynamic place devoted at once to industry and to agriculture, with the vitality of the new and the comfort of the traditional. Soon farming itself was changing. With the Industrial Revolution booming in cities like Boston and Lowell, and people moving by the thousand from farms to cities, a home market for agricultural products was developing for New England farmers. It may be that William Henry Winning's father foresaw the possibilities of a new era in agriculture when he bought the property in Woburn, with far more land than his family's own needs could require. And within a few years, he bought yet more land—also from the Wright family—when he and a relative of his purchased several more acres.

When William Winning was a young child, his mother and older sisters no doubt practiced the traditional arts of spinning and weaving. But by midcentury, many of the products that had been made on the farm, by the farm's women, became available for purchase, thanks to the railroads that were pulling the country into an increasingly tighter network. Soon farm women were being treated to Sunday sermons about the evils of idleness, as the old spinning wheels were retired to the attic, and homespun garments were exchanged for clothing manufactured commercially. Many women across New England left the farm to work in factories, and young men headed out to make their fortunes in the cities. Older folks railed against the heartless departure of youth from family farms, but commentators like Karl Marx saw the new age as "rescuing a considerable part of the population from the idiocy of rural life." Although probably not Marxists, William Winning's siblings joined in the century's grand exodus from farm to city.

William Winning's brother John left Woburn for Fort Plain, New York, where he set up a leather-tanning business. John became head of the local fire department and a wealthy man who was something of a personage in the town.[3] William Winning's sisters were perhaps even more affected by historic changes. All three of them, Nancy Maria, the oldest, Elizabeth P., the middle sister, and William's twin, Lydia, heeded the call of Massachusetts education reformer Horace Mann to become teachers in the newly established public schools.

In times past, rural education had not been altogether neglected, but it was often conducted by lightly educated farmers with time on their hands in the cold months. Now, schools were established to train teachers, and the young Winning women attended the Massachusetts State Normal School in Newton, Massachusetts. Their choice of teaching over factory work or domestic service reflected their social status but did not entirely protect them from exploitation. Equal pay for equal work was not yet dreamed of, as an 1849 comment in the annals of the Littleton (Mass.) School Committee reveals. "It seems... very poor policy," said a committee member, "to pay a man 20 or 22 dollars a month for teaching children the ABCs, when a female could do the work more successfully at one-third of the price."[4]

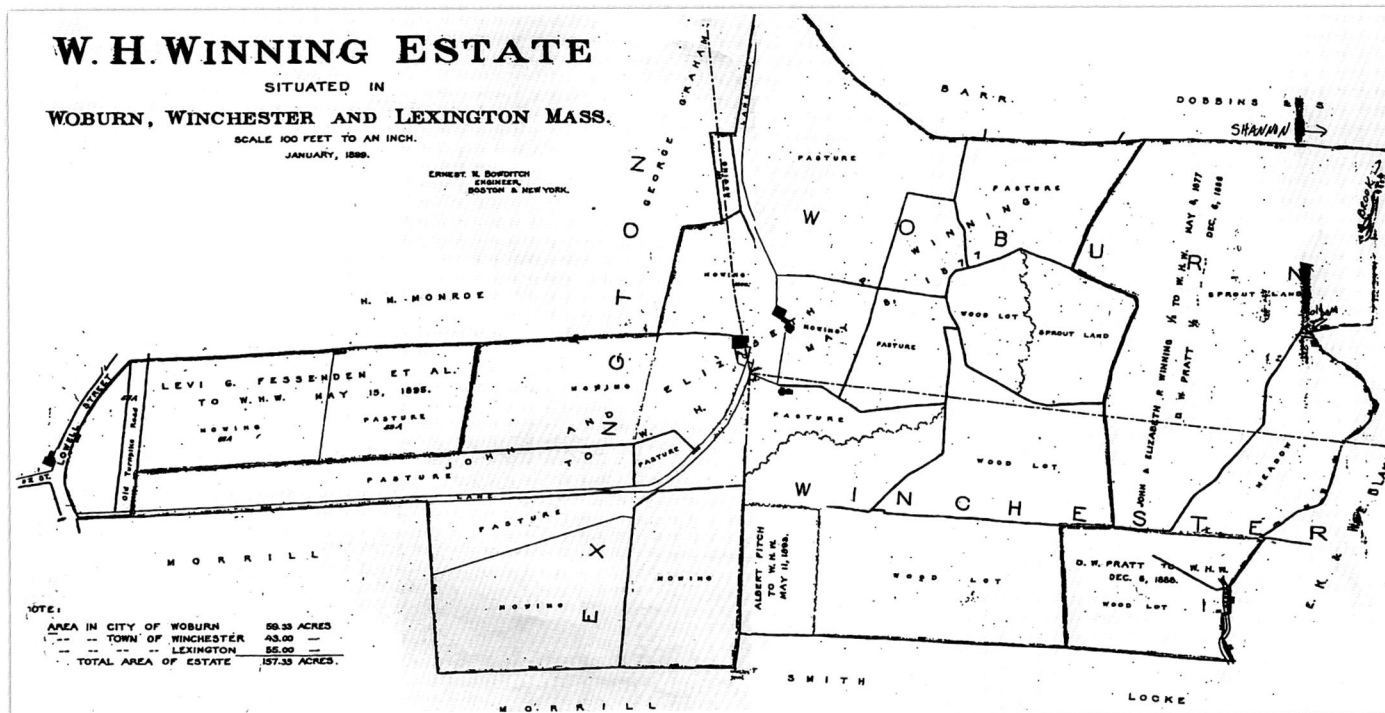

The Winning Estate, 1899. Winning Home Archives

After graduating from normal school and apparently finding work in Boston and Medford, Winning's older sisters—like so many later college graduates—never returned home. His twin sister Lydia did come back to Woburn, where she taught school, but her health was poor, and she died from tuberculosis, the era's great killer, at the age of 30. Winning's other sisters never married, possibly because teachers often lost their jobs if they wed. Why a married woman would be unwelcome in a classroom may be difficult to grasp today, but in many places this prohibition remained in force until the 1960s.[5]

While his siblings looked beyond the farm for their careers, and even broke new ground in pursuing them, William Henry Winning remained at home. He never left Woburn, never left the farm, and never even left the house in which he had been born. But he too was ambitious. His goal, it appears, was to build on his father's success in farming, and the challenges brought by the railroads and other advances of the time seem to have stimulated rather than discouraged him. Many New England farmers in his era actually abandoned their farms and the rocky soil that made farming so difficult in their area. They headed west to create new farms, or joined the modern world of the factory, where wages were poor but predictable, and work was year-round.

Winning, by contrast, expanded his holdings. As indicated on an extant map of the farm, he bought out his siblings in the years following his father's death in 1869, paying them $4,777 for their shares in 1877.[6] When they left the homestead behind for good, he became sole owner of the land his father has purchased in 1830. And he continued to acquire land, not through purchase but through the gifts of relatives on his mother's side, the token $1 being exchanged with the deed. In

1869
*William Henry Winning, age 33,
inherits his father's farm.*

Downtown Woburn in William Winning's time. A horsecar heads south on Main Street at Common Street, 1883. Frank W. Legg, Woburn Public Library, Dexter B. Johnson Collection

1888 he received land from a relative named Fitz. Another donation followed in 1893 by Albert Fitch, a piece of land with a pond on it. In 1895 another land donation, from Levi G. Fessenden.[7] All of these gifts were properties bordering the original farm. One wonders if he planned early on to leave the place to charity and family members wanted to join the effort, or if perhaps he gave these relatives something in exchange for the land. In his will, he would leave many bequests to cousins, perhaps in a kind of repayment.

The farm through William's early years seemed to do well, perhaps in part because his father had given him a good start. When John died in 1869, he left $13,765.45 in cash and personal property and real estate worth $8,182.00,[8] a legacy worth about $471,000 in the early 2020s. In addition to his Woburn farm, he also left land in Chelmsford.

But staying on the farm in these years was a dicey decision. The new industrial era no sooner provided a domestic market in the form of crowded local cities to feed than the railroad began swamping the new markets with produce from farms in western New York state and the Ohio and Mississippi river valleys. New England farmers were forced to respond creatively.

And this William Winning must have done in order to survive and, indeed, to prosper. What did he grow on his farm that worked out well for him? He left no records, and the only answer to this question lies in his map of acquisitions, since it also includes the use of each parcel of land. These parcels were marked "pasture," "wood lot," "meadow," "mowing," and "sprout-land," the last being an area where new growth is harvested from the stumps of trees, a practice that provides access to wood before trees are fully grown. None were marked "cropland."

It's common to think of farms as devoted to growing vegetables or grain. But much of the cleared land in New England was not used for crops. According to one historian, "In the late nineteenth century, only 33 percent of New England farmland was classified as tilled or tillable by the agricultural census. The rest was equally divided between pasture and woodland, with the latter category likely containing much that had once been pasture. In other words, at least half the land ever cleared in New England was pasturage, not cropland, especially on high and rocky ground."[9]

From Winning's map, it can be assumed that "pasture" suggests he grazed a herd of cows. "Meadows" and "mowing" support the growth of hay, a major crop of New England farms in the 19th century, and the basis of food for farm animals. (In the 21st century one still drives past farms in rural New England where hand-lettered signs announce HAY FOR SALE.) We know from other sources that Winning's farm included a cow barn, milk room, icehouse and silo. It appears, then, that his property was largely a dairy farm. This specialization may have kept the farm safer from competition than other choices would have, since refrigerated railroad cars did not yet exist, and dairy farms were thus somewhat insulated from Midwestern competition. Later records suggest that Winning supplemented his dairy investment with a few orchards of apples and peaches, the sale of firewood from areas of woodland and sprout-land, and a certain amount of standard farm produce such as potatoes.

Winning very likely transported this produce to market by horse-drawn wagon. His will notes two wagons, one a one-horse, and one a two-horse. As a local market gardener, he would have taken his wares to Boston's Quincy Market—the regional wholesale market having opened in 1826—as many farmers near the city were known to do. This means that he would load one of his wagons at dusk six nights a week and head into Boston to arrive in the early hours of the morning. Some 21st century farmers, reminiscing for the Woburn Historical Society about farm practices of past times, described a local farmer packing up his wagon in the evening, climbing on board and falling asleep on the seat, while his horse took the wagon to Boston without human guidance. On the way home, the farmer slept again.[10] Saturday night was the farmer's weekly stint in a bed. It was not an easy life.

Children on North Canal island near Pacific Mills, ca. 1896. Courtesy, Lawrence History Center

William Henry Winning
Last Will and Testament 1898

Be it remembered that I, William Henry Winning, of Woburn, in the county of Middlesex and Commonwealth of Massachusetts, make this my Last Will and Testament.

After the payments of my debts and funeral charges, I bequeath and devise as follows:

FIRST: I give to my brother John Winning the sum of two thousand dollars.

SECOND: I give to the following named cousins, provided they survive me and are residents of this Commonwealth at my decease, the sum of one thousand dollars each, namely - Marshall H. Locke of Somerville; Adeline M. Mulliken of Lexington; Augusta R. Buren of Woburn; Ann R. Randall of Worcester; Everett Fitz of Somerville; Charlotte Tufts of Somerville; Susan P. Munroe of Lexington; Julia Winning of Boston; Charlotte Thomas of Stoneham; Martha Harrington of Andover; and Walter Winning of South Chelmsford. But if any of said legatees named in this clause die before I do or shall not be residents of this Commonwealth at the time of my decease, then the legacy as such ones shall lapse and become part of the residue of my estate.

THIRD: I give to Daniel W. Pratt of Winchester the sum of one thousand dollars.

FOURTH: I give to Josephine A. Randall, now of Worcester the sum of one thousand dollars.

FIFTH: I give to Anna H. Roper of Worcester the sum· of one thousand dollars.

SIXTH: I give and devise to Howard M. Munroe of Lexington a part of my Fessenden Place so called, situated in said Lexington, namely, the house and about nine acres of land on the northerly side of Maple Street and the westerly side of Lowell Street and other side, bounded by the Munroe's own land.

SEVENTH: I give and devise to M. Alice Munroe and Elmina Munroe, both of Lexington and in equal shares to each one, that portion of my Fessenden Place so called situated in said Lexington comprising about twenty-five acres with buildings all as now fenced in on the south side of Maple Street and otherwise bounded on the Blodgett place and on the Blanchard place.

EIGHTH: My home place containing about one hundred acres of land with the buildings thereon situated in Woburn, Lexington, and Winchester, and bounded on the south by the Whipple place and by the land of Smith; on the west by Lowell Street, on the north by the land of Howard M. Monroe of Graham; of James Barr and Bobbins and Shannon; and on the east by lands of Hanson of Menchin and of Thompson, I give and devise to John M. Johnson of Woburn, Daniel M. Pratt of Winchester and Howard M. Munroe of Lexington and to their successors in the trust here by created in fee but in trust nevertheless to be used and appropriated for the establishment and maintenance of a home for orphans and other destitute children, either for their permanent or temporary care.

NINTH: All the rest, residue and remainder of my estate, real and personal of which I may die seized or possessed or to which I may be entitled at the time of decease, I give, devise and bequeath in trust to the said John M. Johnson, Daniel M. Pratt, and Howard M. Munroe and their successors in trust to appropriate the net income thereof for the maintenance of said home for orphan and other destitute children as provided for in Article eight of this will.

TENTH: I give to my said trustees, herein named, and to their successors in said trust; full power of the management of the Home, which may be established under the trusts created in this will and I authorize and empower said trustees and such persons as they may select to organize themselves into a corporation, under the laws of the Commonwealth and to convey to such corporation when duly organized all my said trust estate, both real and personal, to be held and managed by said corporation for the purpose of said home and such corporation shall then have full power to manage the funds and direct the affairs of said Home.

ELEVENTH: I authorize and empower my said trustees to sell, exchange and convey at their own discretion all real or personal estate which they may hold under the trusts hereby created, and purchasers from them shall not be answerable for the application of the purchase money.

TWELFTH: The powers herein given to said trustees shall extend to the survivors of them and their successors.

THIRTEENTH: I request that said trustees herein named and their successors who may be appointed by the Probate Court shall be exempt from giving a surety or sureties on their official bond.

FOURTEENTH: I authorize and appoint said John M. Johnson, Daniel M. Pratt and Howard M. Monroe to be executors of this my last will and I request they and each of them be exempt from giving a surety or sureties on their official bond.

FIFTEENTH: I authorize and empower said executors and the survivors and survivor of them to sell, transfer and convey at their own discretion any of my real or personal estate and to execute and deliver proper instrument of transfer and conveyance to the respective purchasers who shall not be answerable for the application of the purchase money.

In witness whereof, I hereunto set may hand and seal and in the presence of three witnesses, declare this to be my last will, this third day of June A.D. 1898

On this third day of June A.D. 1898, William Henry Winning of Woburn, Massachusetts, signed and sealed the foregoing instrument in our presence declaring it to be his last will, and as witness thereof, we three do now at his request, in his presence and in the presence of each other hereto subscribe our names.

Joseph Linnell
Charlie A. Jones
Lottie M. Wyman

William Henry Winning's will as it appeared in a local newspaper.

Hardworking was how a newspaper described William Winning, and he must have been astute and creative as well, to amass a sizable fortune from the farm in the three decades he ran it after his father's passing. It's true his father left him a working farm, along with a certain sum of money. He also left a number of farm implements, including some that were rather dated—an ox cart, ox sled, ox wagon, and three ox yokes, from the time when the mighty ox pulled stumps out of the rocky ground to clear the land. There was also a covered wagon (worth $25 at the time), which sounds odd in the Northeast, but photos of Quincy Market in Boston well into the 20th century show covered wagons in use for hauling produce. They may have been more common on city streets in the East at that time than on long-distance journeys to the West.

So Winning had a head-start from his father's legacy, as well as an early life spent learning the agricultural arts. Still, it was a challenging time to be a farmer in New England, and William came out of it with money to spare. When he sat down in 1898 to write his will, he was able to give $1,000 each to no fewer than 11 cousins and three other individuals. A gift of $1,000 in 1898 would be worth $36,044.58 in the early 21st century.

Winning did stipulate, for reasons unknown, that the cousins be residents of Massachusetts to claim their inheritance. Perhaps it was a kind of reflex Massachusetts jingoism; indeed, future residents of the state were often known to regard the Commonwealth as a generally superior place, and likely the source of the nation's best ideas, from transcendentalism to high technology. But Winning also gave $2,000 to his only surviving sibling, John, who lived in New York, and exempted him from the Massachusetts residency requirement.

The will also bequeathed a house and several acres of land in Lexington to three relatives on his mother's side. And then came the surprise bequest: the residue of his possessions, including his home and more than 100 acres of land, William Winning gave in trust to "John M. Johnson of Woburn, Daniel M. Pratt of Winchester, and Howard M. Munroe of Lexington for the establishment and maintenance of a home for orphans and other destitute children, either for their permanent or temporary care."

Since neither William Henry Winning nor his brother nor any of his three sisters ever married or had children, it might be assumed that Winning's choice of "orphans" and poor children amounted to a conventional charitable gesture. But it may also be that Winning, as a member of a somewhat well-off family, with three educated sisters who had worked in schools, was aware of what was happening to young people in his time.

The population of Boston in 1836, when Winning was born, was 61,000; when he died in 1898, it was 561,000, thanks to farm-to-city migration and immigration from abroad. In Winning's lifetime a rural, agricultural society became an urban society focused on manufacturing—a dramatic change in culture and society that for many children meant early work in factories.

According to "Records of Rights," an exhibit in the U.S. National Archives and Records Administration, "In the early 20th century it was common for children, some as young as four, to work in America's factories, mines, fields, canneries, and tenement sweatshops. By 1910 children under the age of 15 made up 18.4% of the nation's workforce.[11]

October 1898
*William Winning leaves his home and 100-acre farm
in trust for the care of orphans and destitute children.*

The mills of the Industrial Revolution seem far removed from this idyllic scene of Woburn in the 19th century. Lithograph, 1863, Woburn Public Library

Less than 20 miles from his Woburn home, in the mills of Lowell, young children were working long hours. They "were often hurt due to industrial accidents on unsafe machinery, were uneducated since there was no time for school after working more than 12 hours a day, and were infected with illness and disease due to the unsafe working conditions."[12] Child labor laws were still in the future.

Winning wrote his will on June 3, 1898. He would have a health scare, a "shock," said the papers, during the summer. He lived through the early fall and died on October 25, 1898, at the age of 61.

The *Woburn News* summed up his life in a brief obituary dated October 29, 1898: "After the death of Mr. Winning, senior, Wm. H. took the homestead-farm and conducted it successfully. He was a man of sturdy application, finding in his daily work his greatest delight. He had a genial nature and a heart filled with kindness for others, as is evidenced by his unremitting care of his mother while she lived and the beneficent provisions of his last will and testament. Mr. Winning never sought publicity or public station. He was a home-loving and industrious man, a good neighbor and model citizen."

CHAPTER TWO

Reverend Perin's Summer Camp:
A now-forgotten social reformer, a great fundraiser, an impressive leader, a man of his time

William Winning's farm may well have become an orphanage. Indeed, the wording of his will—the reference to "permanent" care of orphans—suggested this possibility. With a few alterations, his spacious home could have readily accommodated a dozen young people, and many children in 1900 needed homes. Conditions in nearby cities, packed with immigrants from southern and eastern Europe living in crowded neighborhoods with high rates of tuberculosis and frequent epidemics of typhoid and cholera, produced many parentless children. The farm might offer a new home, a long-term refuge from a troubled world.

But orphanages were coming under heavy criticism as the 19th century drew to a close. Children were subjected to severe regimentation and harsh conditions in institutions that were only a step up from poor houses, which in turn were essentially prisons. One mid-century reformer, so-called, came up with the drastic scheme of putting urban orphans on trains, sending them to the midwest, and letting farm families choose them on sight. Some children fared well through this process; others slipped into a kind of slavery.[13]

But the farm did not become an orphanage. It became, instead, a summer camp, focused on the alternative in Winning's will, which called for either "permanent or temporary" care of needy children. In becoming a summer camp, Winning Home caught a new wave in the care of urban children, providing a relief from the ills of city life,

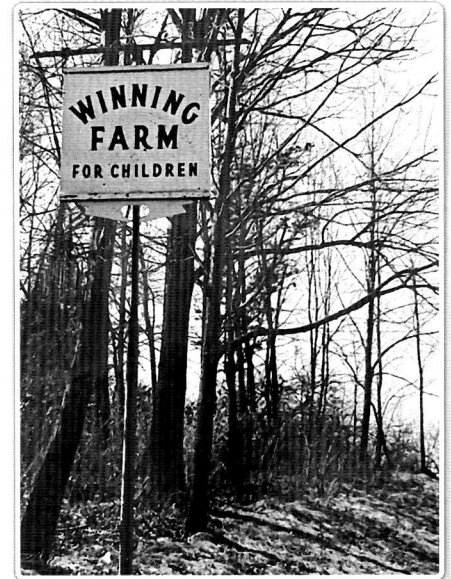

"What a noble use to which to donate one's property! The high elevation of this spot with its fine outlook, the advantages of wholesome food, pure water and outdoor exercise, the minimum of transportation expense and the complete change of scene and environment will work wonders with the thin and wasted, pale and sickly, ill-fed and half-nourished children of the poor from the urban streets."

–Woburn News, June 16, 1900

WINNING FARM SONG

By Rev. Charles Forest Barter

Far from the city's heat and noise
There stands a lovely home,
Where many happy girls and boys
In the summer months may roam.
A breeze from heaven bathes the brows
of children gathered there,
And fills their hearts with praise and love
For the country home so fair.

(Chorus)
O Winning Farm, thy praise I sing!
I hold thy memory dear,
I love thy flowers and waving trees,
Thy woodlands far and near.
Thy hills and valleys fertile green
Will never lose their charm,
My heart shall sing its love for thee,
Three cheers for Winning Farm!

The days go by in happy play,
The childish heart is free,
Sweet mem'ries form for later years
Wherever they may be.
The birds make merry in the trees,
The flowers bloom for all,
With song they greet the morning sun,
With praise the twilight's fall.

The Winning Farm Song, written in 1904.

attempting to boost their health with good food and abundant milk, and giving them a taste of a different existence by transporting them for a week or more to a rural environment, far from the city streets.

Summer camping was in fact the trend of the moment. In 1900 there were about 100 summer camps in the United States; by 1918 there were over 1,000. Launched in the 1880s in Europe, summer camps represented a reaction against the developments of the 19th century that brought so many rural residents to the city and so profoundly changed the way people lived.

A popular idea at the turn of the century that would shape those camps into the future was that children grew through stages that recapitulated the history of the human race. Many were cheated of the early stage, regarded as a primitive, carefree period in life, by being forced into work in urban settings. At camp, then, young people built fires for warmth and cooking and spent days out of doors, swimming and hiking, and—at the very moment industrialization was turning out machine-made goods—learning to make useful things by hand. Early camping was also influenced by the "fresh air" movement and the playground movement of the late 19th century, recognitions that urban life could be damaging to children's health and that children were not just young workers but individuals with different needs from adults.[14]

Perhaps even more fundamental to the development of camping was the change in attitude toward nature that came about as people moved into urban environments. Poetry in the early 19th century found a deeper meaning in nature, and philosophic writers such as Emerson and Thoreau helped replace the traditional image of nature as dangerous and unsparing with the idea of nature as humanity's true home. The majestic vistas of the Hudson River School artists presented nature not as something to be conquered but as something with healing powers and sacred implications. The idea of spending time in a natural environment began to acquire a new and very different significance as, according to one historian, "interest in America's landscape began to acquire spiritual and symbolic dimensions."[15]

Against this deep background summer camping became the mission of the newly created organization, and the three men Winning appointed as trustees set about converting the old farmhouse for a new use—which required some work. According to Winning Home records, "The only plumbing in the house was a kitchen sink and hand pump. The water used at the house was supplied by a small cistern, which stored a portion of roof water, and two wells, one of which was located in front of the house and the other at the cow barn."[16]

The trustees made repairs and did some serious renovating. According to the *Woburn News* on June 16, 1900, "The two upper stories are being fitted as dormitories, and when completed will show 20 to 25 rooms, each say 5 x 9 ft divided by moveable partitions and fitted with swing doors. Each child will have a room by itself. A generous 20 x 25 foot addition has been built, which will be used as a dining room." The paper added that the goal was to have 20 children at a time for a stay of two weeks over the summer months in order "to secure a needed release from the foulness of the congested district."

The newspaper estimated the cost of the renovations at $5,000. The necessary funds came from Winning's legacy. In addition to the farmhouse and surrounding acres, Winning had left several bank accounts yielding interest, six real estate mortgages he held for other people, personal property consisting of several cows, a horse, farm implements, and securities, altogether valued at $31,797.59 at the time of his death. After the will was settled in January 1900, the trustees had $28,542.25 to cover the renovations and launch the new venture.[17]

Finally it was time to determine who would operate the camping program. The trustees were gratified to secure the services of George L. Perin (1854-1921), the pastor of the Universalist church at 397 Shawmut Avenue in Boston. They looked to him to organize the camp, hire counselors and other employees, locate the children and escort them from the city to the farm. Reverend Perin proved a fortunate choice in many ways, not the least of which being the status and recognition he brought to the new endeavor.

Raised on a dairy farm in Iowa, Perin had become a major figure in Boston for his charismatic preaching and creative philanthropic enterprises. When he arrived in the city near the turn of the century,

Taking a ride with one of the farm's gentle horses, 1908. Courtesy, Theodora Ballard, Winning Home Archives

jobs were opening for women but low pay forced them to live in rundown boarding houses in high-crime parts of town. Sensing their plight, Perin purchased the former St. James Hotel, once the most luxurious hotel in the city. With his great capacity as a fundraiser, Perin managed to turn the former hotel into a highly successful and even famous undertaking, which the *New York Times* in 1913 called "the largest hotel for young working women and girl students in the world." Located in Boston's South End, the Franklin Square House, with a capacity of 850 residents, served as a reasonably priced home for single women through much of the 20th century, providing not only safe accommodations but lectures, concerts, and a variety of supportive programs. It survives in the 21st century as affordable housing.[18]

It was this work in which Perin was engaged when Winning Home tapped him to run its new summer camping program. "No better man could have been selected," said the *Woburn News* on June 16, 1900. "He has a practical, common sense understanding of the needs of Boston's poor children." Toward the first summer's camping, the trustees set aside $800, and Perin immediately launched a fundraising program that reflected his flair for publicity. An appeal in the *Winchester Star* on July 15, 1902, pointed out that 250 children who had been invited for the summer were "anxiously awaiting their turn to go. One-third of them will have to be disappointed unless immediate contributions are sent in. Will not the people of this town [Winchester] respond? Any gift from $1 to $50 will be gladly received." A few days later, another notice added that "just $2.50 gives one child a week's 'paradise.'"

The promise of paradise brought in substantial funds, and Perin was able to transport children to the farm and create a raft of activities for them. By the summer of 1900, the camp at Winning Farm was in full swing, with 180 children attending. Initially, the children were "boarded out" to families in the area, according to the *Boston Globe*, but by 1901 the

newly renovated farmhouse provided accommodations. At the end of the 1903 season, the number of children attending was up to 252, including 161 girls and 91 boys. Reverend Perin proudly proclaimed the various backgrounds represented in terms of religion, ethnicity and race. The 271 children who attended in one of those early years included "91 Catholic, 22 Jewish, and 158 Protestants. Nearly every nationality has been represented, and while the groups are usually of [racially] mixed children, one whole week was devoted to children [of color]."

The farm continued to prosper. In June 23, 1905, a newspaper reported, "This is the sixth year that the Trustees of the property have given the use of the farmhouse to Dr. Perin, and he intends to fill it up again this summer with a crowd of happy boys and girls from the poorer quarters of Boston."[19]

Perin's flair for publicity, along with his personal popularity in Boston, attracted extensive coverage. The newspapers loved the image of a farm full of happy children. The *Boston Globe* published photos of children riding in a hay wagon, making ice cream and milking cows—with girls dressed in overalls—and described the farm as "an ideal place for a vacation. A perfectly delightful big square white country house commands a view of miles of cultivated land, hills and meadows, sparkling rivers and luxuriant trees... There are green lawns and groves of trees with swings hanging from immense elms and maples, and here high carnival is held all day long by the little visitors from the smoky, dusty city."[20]

Part of the attraction of the farm for children—as well as for newspaper reporters—was that the place so perfectly embodied an idyll of rural life. It is "a real farm," sighed the *Globe*, "with hills and berry pastures, and any quantity of fresh milk and vegetables, and grass to roll about in, and shady nooks and pleasant groves which are just the place for picnics. There are trees to climb and a delightful barn to play in. Swings

October 1900
Winning Farm opens with 180 children participating.

THE BOSTON GLOBE—SATURDAY, AUGUST 12, 1905.

HAPPY SUMMER DAYS AT WINNING FARM

Hospitable Old New England Home Where Poor Children from the City Enjoy a Week's Vacation—Last Year 271 Were Entertained—Piazza Greatly Needed.

A RIDE IN THE HAY RACK

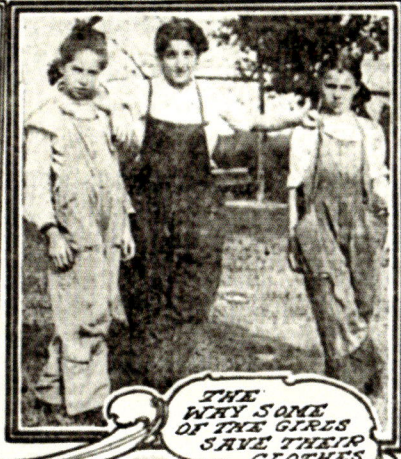

THE WAY SOME OF THE GIRLS SAVE THEIR CLOTHES

LOU L. HEATON WHOM THE CHILDREN CALL "POP"

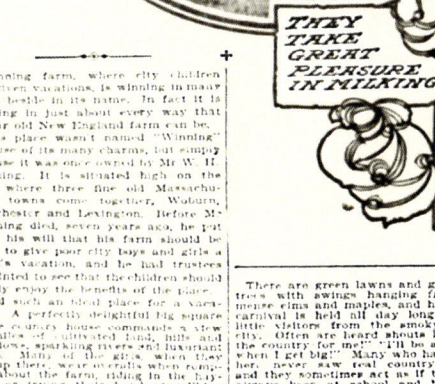

THEY TAKE GREAT PLEASURE IN MILKING

MAKING ICE CREAM

THE FARM HOUSE.

Winning farm, where city children are given vacations, is winning in many ways beside in its name. In fact it is winning in just about every way that a dear old New England farm can be.

This place wasn't named "Winning" because of its many virtues, but simply because it was once owned by Mr W. H Winning. It is situated high on the hills where three fine old Massachusetts towns come together, Woburn, Winchester and Lexington. Before Mr Winning died, seven years ago, he put it in his will that his farm should be used to give poor city boys and girls a week's vacation, and he had trustees appointed to see that the children should surely enjoy the benefits of the place.

And such an ideal place for a vacation! A perfectly delightful big square white country house commands a view of miles of cultivated land, hills and meadows, sparkling rivers and luxuriant trees. Many of the girls, when they get up there, wear overalls when romping about the farm, riding in the hayrick or trying their hand at milking the clever old cow.

The farm is exactly at the point where the three towns named come together, for, while all the buildings are within a stone's throw of one another, the house is in Woburn, the barn in Lexington and the farm cottage in Winchester. A granite monument on the farm indicates the lines of the different towns.

There are green lawns and groves of trees with swings hanging from immense elms and maples, and here high carnival is held all day long by the little visitors from the smoky, dusty city. Often are heard shouts like: "Oh, the country for me!" "I'll be a farmer when I get big!" Many who have come here never saw real country before, and they sometimes act as if they had always been at school and had just been let out for the first time in their lives.

The boys have the farm to themselves a week, then the girls come for a week. It is pleasant to see that they don't forget those of the family who couldn't come, for it is a common thing, when they return home, for them to take a large basket of berries to father or mother or to other youngsters.

The trustees have the privilege of delegating the outing work to any church organization they may select, and for the last seven years, ever since the work was begun, the Every-Day church, of which Dr George L. Perin was pastor, and his successor, the Beacon Universalist church of Brookline, has had charge of the project. Dr Perin, the present pastor of the last-named church, has general supervision. Through his church paper, the Beacon Light, which has a circulation of about 2000 copies and hundreds of private letters written to his friends, a fund is raised sufficient to pay the expenses of 11-weeks' outings each summer. Dr Perin redoubled his efforts this summer, and $900 was contributed, which enabled the trustees to continue the outings for three months, commencing in June and continuing until the schools open in September. The Young People's organization of the Beacon church is in charge of the summer work, and Thomas Pollitt, treasurer of the society, is also treasurer of the fund.

There are accommodations for 25 each week. Lou L. Heaton, the superintendent, himself a young man, having been graduated last June from St Lawrence college, Canton, N Y, is very popular with the boys and girls, entering heartily into all their games and directing them in any work they wish to take up.

Winning farm, which is highly cultivated, contains 120 acres. Farmer Walker attends to the farm the year round and not only grows good things for the youthful visitors to eat, but raises some produce for sale. There is a fine herd of cattle, including 21 milch cows, and the dairy is said to be one of the best in that section. Mr Walker is particularly proud of his orchard, which last year produced over 80 barrels of the best quality of apples. Hundreds of quarts of all kinds of berries are also grown.

The visitors come from all over Boston, and their ages range from five to 15 years. They are of all sects, and there is no prohibition on account of race or color. The nationalities represented, so far this season, have been English, Irish, Jewish, American, Hungarian, Swedish, Armenians. If there should be representatives of several denominations in one week, Mr Heaton consults their wishes, and usually they go to the church which is represented by the majority. None is compelled to attend services at any church, but all are expected to say grace before meals. The food is plain, but wholesome, and there is plenty of it. About 100 quarts of milk are consumed every day, and there is an abundance of eggs, butter and ice cream.

The only drawback pointed out in the house was the absence of a piazza. This is very much needed, as on wet days the reception rooms and parlor are overtaxed. A piano is one of the attractions, and many of the children play or sing.

13

and hammocks there are in plenty and games for stormy days and a piano to use for the 'sings.'" [21]

Not only was the place a real farm, it had a real farmer. As the *Globe* story noted, "Farmer Walker attends to the farm the year round, and not only grows good things for the youthful visitors to eat, but raises some produce for sale." In fact, Winning Home's records from the early years of summer camping indicate that the farm received income from the sale of cranberries, apples, milk, wood and potatoes. "There is a fine herd of cattle," the *Globe* continued, "including 21 milch cows, and the dairy is said to be one of the best in that section. Mr. Walker is particularly proud of his orchard, which last year produced over 80 barrels of the best quality of apples. Hundreds of quarts of all kinds of berries are also grown." [22]

Many stories stressed the abundance of food provided for children whose families often lacked adequate nourishment. "The food is plain, but wholesome, and there is plenty of it. [Many] quarts of milk are consumed every day, and there is an abundance of eggs, butter and ice cream."

An injection of support for the farm came in 1905 with one of Winning Home's rare legacies subsequent to William Winning's original bequest. Winning's older brother John died in Fort Plain, New York. "A conspicuous figure at firemen's conventions throughout the state," according to his obituary in the *Boston Evening Transcript*, John (who stood 6'7") had served as chief of the local fire department. "He went to Fort Plain in 1860 to engage in the tanning business, in which he acquired a fortune." With no immediate heirs, he left sums to various relatives, but his largest bequest, $8,000, went to Winning Farm. [23]

Reverend Perin contributed his talents to Winning Farm for six years, establishing the new program and setting the pattern of a prestigious institution operating the summer camp at the farm. In 1906, he

relinquished his role in the program, for reasons unknown, but the history of the Franklin Square House, and the demanding job of raising funds to meet its hefty $250,000 purchase price, likely consumed his energy, considerable as it was. As a consequence, Winning Farm, after just a few years in operation, had to search for a new organization to operate the summer camping program. Meanwhile the *Boston Globe* continued sending reporters out to Woburn to bring back good news about childhood in a time when many young people were working long hours in factories and living in squalid tenements.

"The boys and girls take different turns going," wrote the *Globe* in one of those early summers, "and are allowed to romp and play to their hearts' content among apple orchards and barns and clover fields and all the other spots that give pleasure to the town child in the country." [24]

Tenement Alley, Boston. Photo by Lewis Hine. Courtesy of the George Eastman Museum

Winning Farm and the Settlement House Movement:
A national leader, an effort to redefine poverty, a refuge from the urban wilderness

The *Globe*'s idyllic description of young folks romping on their own in the country was not what Robert A. Woods, the head of the South End House in Boston, had in mind for children. Instead of "merely…letting children loose amid rural scenes," he wrote to the farm's trustees, "we have worked continuously to develop all the educational possibilities of such outings." When the South End House took over the operation of Winning Farm's camping program in the summer of 1906, Woods brought an element of rigor and purpose to what had been a simple summer vacation for impoverished urban children.[25]

Like Reverend Perin, Woods was well known in Boston. In fact, he had a national reputation as one of the leading figures in the settlement house movement in America. He had come to Boston in 1889 and established the city's first settlement house, the South End House, which is still in existence in the 21st century as part of United South End Settlements (USES). Woods wrote several authoritative books on the movement.

Settlement houses offered job training in handicrafts. Here, women practice sewing at Denison House, Boston, 1915.College Settlement Association Quarterly, vol 1, no. 1.

It was a movement that generated excitement similar to that of the Peace Corps of the 1960s, with a powerful attraction for recent college graduates, including the many women who were becoming educated but for whom few jobs existed. The movement grew over the next several years to approximately 500 settlement houses nationwide. As an institution it was to prove key to the development of social work in the United States, and through settlement volunteers like Frances Perkins, who became Franklin Roosevelt's secretary of labor, an important influence on the development of Social Security and related government-supported social services. Another settlement house volunteer, Eleanor Roosevelt, would prove even more influential in developing government policies in the 1930s and '40s when her husband was President and thereafter as an independent political figure.

Equally focused on providing services and promoting reform, the settlement movement hoped to remove the moral stigma of poverty. Settlement houses provided job training and English language classes and conducted studies that served as the bases of legislation to improve conditions in poor neighborhoods. They established "milk stations" at a time when much milk available in cities was unsafe to drink; they set up public baths when many tenement buildings lacked bathing facilities entirely; they created dispensaries in areas where healthcare was largely unavailable; and they provided services such as emergency loan and savings programs in communities experiencing extreme poverty as a result of low wages. In addition, they developed free concerts, art exhibitions, reading rooms, and a variety of social, dramatic and literary clubs at a time when impoverished urban areas lacked cultural amenities of any kind.

Woods's settlement house was in Boston's South End, then the city's poorest neighborhood, populated by immigrants living in unsanitary, unsafe and overcrowded housing, where disease was rampant. Many of the poor, including young children, worked 12- and 14-hour days in factories for scant wages.

In 1906, the South End House launched a partnership with Winning Home that would last more than half a century. The settlement house brought children to the farm and provided the overall philosophic and practical framework of the summer camping program, while Winning Home provided the location, physical structures, outdoor spaces, and farm experience. Directors of the South End House, including Robert A. Woods, became board members of Winning Home, and Winning Home was likewise represented on the board of the settlement house. Winning Home's annual meetings were sometimes held in Boston at the settlement house headquarters and other times at the farm or at a bank in downtown Woburn.

The South End House employed a dietician at the farm to help improve the health of the campers. The farm's own fresh food and especially its milk were a plus, given the fact that, according to a 1907 Fannie Farmer cookbook, much milk at the time was watered down and whitened with the addition of chalk and food dyes.[26] Early board meetings were devoted to decisions about cows, including which breeds were more desirable and how much should be paid for them. Children, often hungry at home, ate well at the farm, which continued producing crops for several decades. To assure the supply of fresh food, the board set aside $3,000 to construct a cottage to house a permanent farmer. The structure was dedicated to William Winning's brother John, in honor of his early bequest to the farm.

Reflecting Woods's concern about education, the staff included two counselors, one an expert in bird life and the other in flowers, to take the children through the woods, pointing out specimens of animal and plant life.

At the farm, said a newspaper, the children all had a room of their own, whereas at home they often slept three or more to a bed. And the farm was full of interesting things—fields and meadows of grasses and wild flowers, berries for the picking, farm implements and farm wagons, and farm animals including horses, cattle, sheep, goats and chickens, not to mention the wood lots, with extensive stands of trees. One young camper said she had never seen a tree before. Another said she'd never seen a sunset. One newspaper story reported that the children cried when it was time to go back home.

At times the South End House arranged visits and vacations for adults in addition to the camping experiences for children. As reported in the *Boston Evening Transcript* on July 11, 1912, for example, "The Milk and Baby Hygiene Association sent another little group of mothers with their babies today to the Winning Farm in Lexington for a ten-day vacation. A cottage at the farm has been placed at the disposal of the Baby Hygiene Association for this purpose. The first group of mothers and infants to be sent there returned yesterday and the vacancies were filled today. This will be continued through the hot season."[27]

1906–1965

Boston's South End House administers the summer camping program at Winning Farm.

Time for lights out, August 1952. Patrick J. Farino. Courtesy, Woburn Public Library, Glennon Archives

Making ice cream, August 1952. Patrick J. Farino. Woburn Public Library, Glennon Archives

Playing dress-up, 1961. William T. Ryerson. Winning Home Archives

But camping was the primary activity of the South End House at Winning Farm over the years and was popular with children and their parents. From early on, the children's parents, despite their low incomes, helped defray the cost of the camping program, paying $7 for a two-week stay for each child, an amount later reduced to $6. But no one was turned away. The South End House helped subsidize the program through their men's club Saturday night whist parties, which brought in $200 a year.

Winning's legacy continued to produce substantial income from mortgages and investments, but the expense of running the farm was climbing. World War I pushed up the cost of labor. "In 1916, due to the prevailing war conditions, Italian farm laborers were asking $2.85 per day commencing at 8 o'clock each morning instead of 7 o'clock as formerly." In addition, Winning Home was now supporting a full-time farmer for $75 a month. There was also the expense of a year-round caretaker.

While newspapers described "a glorious summer vacation" from "a crowded Hub tenement district to a countryside estate surrounded by nature's beauty," Winning Farm's board of directors, which raised its contribution to the settlement house year by year, worried about costs. The board produced a document called "A Brief Review of the Work Done at Winning Home 1898-1918," which summed up their concerns, including what became a perennial refrain regarding "year-round" vs. "summer-only" programming. [28]

"We still had in mind that we were not accomplishing the work that we understood Mr. Winning intended to have done," said the report. "It was realized that in order to maintain all-the-year home for children, our finances were insufficient."

Outside of income from investments and the sale of produce, support to the farm came from just two sources in those first 20 years—John

Swinging at the farm, ca. 1961. William T. Ryerson. Winning Home Archives

Having fun on the carousel, 1961. William T. Ryerson. Winning Home Archives

Winning's substantial bequest of $8,000 in 1905, and another bequest from a man named George Swain in 1914. Swain, from a prosperous family in Wilmington, was a compulsive borrower of other people's horses, and years in prison didn't cure him of the habit; in his lifetime he stole more than a thousand horses, often including buggies. He would take horses from livery stables, drive them to the next town, and abandon them. But he never lacked for money from his family and when he died he left $1,000 to the farm to help fund vacations for Boston children. [29]

Concern over finances was the likely reason the farm turned to its fundamental asset, the land itself. In 1923, the board sold 46.5 acres to Harvey C. Wheeler for $150 an acre, for a total price of $6,975. Mr. Wheeler paid $2,500 in cash and the farm provided a mortgage at seven percent for the balance—a fairly high rate in the 1920s, when bank mortgage rates averaged four to five percent. [30]

This was only a temporary solution, of course, and financial worries continued to nag at the board. Nevertheless, the farm maintained its

camping program for boys and girls from the South End of Boston for decades to come.

And the respite from an impoverished life for children in the city would continue to be needed. During the Great Depression of the 1930s, with 25 percent unemployment, many middle class families slipped into poverty, producing increased hunger and malnutrition among children. The Depression does not appear as such in Winning Home's records except in the form of a Works Progress Administration (WPA) project in the 1930s to clear a drainage ditch and lay a pipe in its place, but the farm's abundant and nourishing food was more important than ever to the young campers who came for a few weeks in the summer.

Major issues such as wars seemed remote from the quiet hills and meadows of Winning Farm, and were felt only minimally during World War II. But one does see in the lists of counselors a woman named Thelma Ham, who had worked in France during the summer of 1939 in a camp for refugees of the Spanish Civil War and was among

Feeding the farm animals, 1961. William T. Ryerson. Winning Home Archives

the American passengers on the last ship to leave France before the German occupation.[31]

In 1944, the South End House marked its 50th anniversary with a report that celebrated its many contributions to the South End neighborhood. "One of the group activities of which the House is most justly proud is its camp work," the report said. "Two camps are conducted," one in New Hampshire and the other in Massachusetts. "The Winning Farm Camp in Woburn, about 15 miles from Boston,…is a very simple camp on a quiet old estate with woods and fields. It is used for the younger boys and girls of our neighborhoods, usually those between 6 and 13 years of age. Emphasis has been placed upon a relaxing un-regimented program, but one which nevertheless is aimed at developing a high degree of self-sufficiency and appreciation of simple recreational and cultural pursuits."[32]

After the war, through the 1950s, children continued to come to the farm, although it was now girls-only, where previously boys and girls alternated. The board determined that boys were well served by other camps at this point and that Winning Farm would focus on girls.

In these years, when crime among young people began to be called juvenile delinquency, the farm earned special praise. Winning Home's annual meeting minutes from 1956 cite a prominent local judge's "sincere approval of the constructive work that was done by the Winning Farm Camp for Girls in these days of widespread juvenile delinquency, when many people are talking about what should be done to solve the problems whereas such organizations as the South End House and…the Winning Farm for Girls actually are doing something constructive to prevent juvenile delinquency before it occurs."

But changing times seemed not to mar the deep pleasures of young people camping at the old farm, where days in the 1950s and '60s were not very different from days in the 1920s. Whatever was happening in the larger world, the camping day at Winning Farm represented a rare kind of permanence. At 7 a.m. the girls ate breakfast as a group and then returned to their rooms to straighten up and make their beds. Next came swimming. With no lake of its own, Winning Farm transported campers to Foley Beach at Woburn's Horn Pond, or to Walden Pond in Concord, for a two-hour swimming lesson. Then came the mid-day meal followed by a rest period. In the afternoon it was time for arts and crafts. The campers made such items as beaded pocketbooks, beanies, handkerchiefs, paintings and woodcraft to display on visiting day to parents. After the evening meal there was the campfire and stories from the counselors as darkness settled down on the woods. Finally, the end-of-the-day ceremony with old camp songs and at last, taps. Then off to bed.[33]

The powerful appeal of these days away from the modern world did not diminish with time. In its reports the South End House described the farm as "a paradise for outdoor programs and experiences. The topography was well suited for nature expeditions, woodland games, reptile and animal hunts and rock collections." And then there were the farm's animals—an early petting zoo. "A unique aspect of the camp is its corral with its friendly assortment of goats, baby calves, a wooly lamb, little ducks and big ducks, hens and rabbits," a South End House report noted. "Feeding and caring for the animals is part of camp life. Giving the lamb a bath, gathering eggs or helping to wean the calves are all never-to-be-forgotten experiences."[34]

Despite the sense of permanence surrounding the camping experience, rising costs in the 1950s began to threaten the viability of the farm's work with children. The South End House now estimated a weekly price tag of $1,000 for the camping program, which served 45 girls a week for three sessions of three-week vacations. It was at this point that the Winchester Rotary Club pitched in to help.

1950s
Winning Farm becomes exclusively for girls.

Calling home, August 1952. Patrick J. Farino. Woburn Public Library, Glennon Archives

"It was quite a sight to see bankers, lawyers, and other assorted white-collar types turning to all manner of trades to complete the project," wrote the Rotary Club's Jack Kean of the club's work at the farm. "They were masons, painters, carpenters and apprentices." They built five cabins—"18-by-20-foot buildings designed by Rotarian Bailey Foster… with partially screened-in walls to permit maximum fresh air." [35] The cabins made for more comfortable sleeping accommodations for the campers, who previously slept in the attic of the main house.

The men built a 20-foot-square concrete wading pool and installed swings, sandboxes, a shuffleboard court, and a carousel that would become a part of the farm's lore. They also remodeled the kitchen and put in an industrial dishwasher. [36]

Others who offered to help included members of the 101st Engineer Battalion of the Army National Guard—Headquarters and B Companies—who "worked hard making proper surveys of the farm, constructing roads, bridging brooks, building culverts and laying out a proper drainage system." They even built "a new main road to the farm from Lexington Street in Woburn." They would report to the farm "with bulldozers, shovels, trucks, and other construction equipment, . . . part of the work being intended to give them practical experience." [37]

The assistance of the Winchester Rotary Club reflected a new level of community activism in the 1950s, the era of backyard barbecues and PTA meetings, when the suburbs came to be regarded as an ideal place to raise a family. For Winning Home the outburst of local support and voluntarism presaged the farm's transformation into an organization that would draw on the surrounding community for help and focus its services on local children. Indeed, within a few years, the half-century-long relationship between Winning Farm and the South End House would dissolve, as one chapter in the farm's history came to a close and another opened.

CHAPTER FOUR

The Boys Club:
Winning Home becomes a local organization

"This may seem like a bold request, but I feel it is well founded," wrote John M. McFadden, executive director of the Boys Club of Woburn, to Winning Home on January 22, 1965. "I would like to meet with the Board of Directors of Winning Home, Inc., to discuss the possibility of the Woburn Boys Club administering the Winning Farm Camp. We would guarantee every deserving youngster in our area a memorable camping experience at little or no cost."

It was indeed a bold move considering that the South End House had been administering the program since 1906 and the Woburn Boys Club had just opened its doors in 1964, and that the campers had always been drawn from Boston's South End, whereas the current proposal would serve children from Woburn, Lexington, Winchester and possibly Burlington. It would be a dramatic change. But the Boys Club was a new venture, full of energy and plans. Serving children from a broad spectrum of incomes, it included Winning Home's constituency of low-income children within its purview.

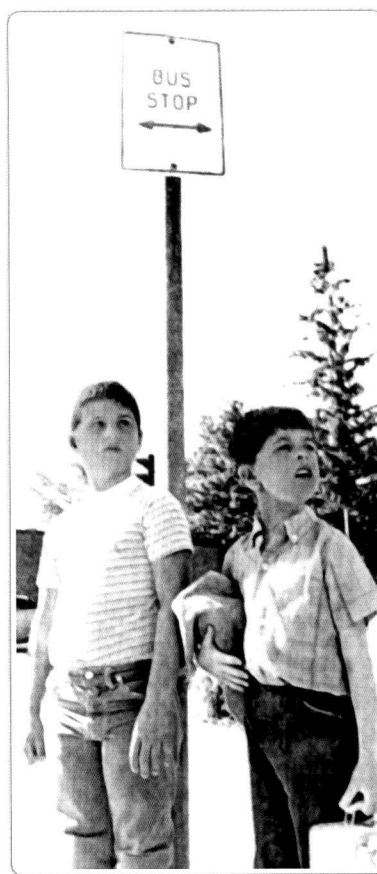

The change was perhaps a recognition that needy children were not confined to big cities. "We have many children in our area currently on the rolls of Aid to [Families with] Dependent Children," McFadden pointed out. The existence of poverty in the suburbs was becoming more evident, a phenomenon that would escalate in the near future. Within a few decades, according to a Rockefeller Foundation study, there would be "more poor people in the United States living in suburbs than in cities, and . . . the growth rate of suburban poverty was significantly outpacing the growth rate of urban poverty." [38]

McFadden felt strongly that there was a need to be served in Woburn and surrounding communities and he approached Winning Home's board with enthusiasm. He pointed out that, in working with the Boys Club, Winning Home could serve children year-round rather than just in the summer—a long held but elusive goal of the organization.

Heading for camp, Woburn Daily Times, *1970. Winning Home Archives*

May 1965
Winning Farm accepts Woburn Boys Club's offer to administer the camping program.

Like the South End House, the Woburn Boys Club had ties to a national organization with a long history. The first Boys Club was founded in 1860 in Hartford, Connecticut, by Elizabeth Hammersley, Louisa Bushnell, Mary Goodwin and Alice Goodwin. It joined a number of other independent Boys' Clubs in 1906 to become the Federated Boys' Clubs and in 1931 renamed itself the Boys' Clubs of America. In 1990 it would become the Boys & Girls Clubs of America. By the early 21st century the organization would include over 4,000 autonomous local clubs serving four million girls and boys nationwide and be ranked as the top youth organization in the country by the *Chronicle of Philanthropy.*

Launched in 1964, the Woburn Boys Club, which would become the Woburn Boys & Girls Club in 1992, quickly became a magnet for local children, offering many of them a place to go after school for recreation—with its gym and swimming pool—and for educational opportunities. Ever-expanding programs meant that a club member could get help with homework or learn cooking, computer coding, acting, photography, card games, or watercolor painting; they could write their own ending to a literary classic, or even discover why bananas are good conductors of electricity. Along the way, young people could learn how to deal with others in an environment of supportive adults. Within a dozen available activities, they could also choose what they wanted to do with their time, an important opportunity for decision-making in the sometimes over-scheduled life of modern childhood. [39]

The club would leave an indelible mark on the lives of many local boys and girls. Interviewed in 2023, Joseph Gaiero, a staff member of the Boys & Girls Club, says he came to the club as a young person initially for sports and socializing. For him the Boys Club experience was so absorbing that he feels it shaped his young life. "Was it a second home?" he asked. "Almost a first." Often arriving right after school and staying until dinner time, he would likely return after the evening meal. A committed and deeply involved member of the club, Joe eventually earned the prized title Boy of the Year, the organization's most prestigious honor. [40]

Back in the 1960s it was partly a coincidence that fueled the Boys Club take-over of programming at the farm. Early in the decade the South End House began pressing Winning Home to build a swimming pool on the site—the very amenity that the new Boys Club had to offer, and one that Winning Home itself did not have the financial resources to supply. By May 1965, after the South End House announced that it would not be holding day camp at the farm that year because of poor enrollment, Winning Home made the decision to part ways with the settlement house and accept the Boys Club's offer to administer activities at the farm. Summer would extend into winter now, and there might be skiing, ice skating and ice sculptures.

After decades of successful collaboration with the South End House, the transition seemed abrupt, but the Boys Club brought new energy along with new plans and generated a wave of excitement that drew a new generation of young people from the surrounding area to the farm. Over the next several years, newspapers reflected the success of the venture. "Winning Farm is Flourishing," trumpeted the *Woburn Daily Times* in early June of 1975. "We figure we had about 8,000 persons here last year," said Charles Murphy of Winchester, chair of the executive committee of Winning Home and a major force driving the new era. Board President Thomas J. Martin III added, "The place is used every weekend year-round." [41]

Sliding into home, June 9, 1977. Woburn Daily Times. *Winning Home Archives*

1975
Winning Farm is at its peak of activity–8,000 boys served.

Learning archery, August 3, 1978. Don Young. Woburn Daily Times. *Winning Home Archives*

Enthusiastic support came from local organizations. "The Woburn Kiwanis Club has taken a tremendous interest in the area," the newspaper noted. In fact the Kiwanians, in one of their many contributions to the farm, had moved a disused real estate building from Woburn's Four Corners to the farm, created a foundation for it, refurbished it to serve as a cabin for camping activities and dedicated it on November 2, 1974, to the memory of T.J. Martin, a long-time supporter of Winning Home. The paper reported that "805 boys enjoyed the camp in four different two-week periods" the previous year, and the number was expected to grow. Together, the service clubs (Woburn Kiwanis and Winchester Rotary) supplied more than 47 camperships to needy boys," said the paper. Other groups offered assistance as well. The Northeast Regional Vocational School restored the restrooms in the main house, built new picnic tables, and developed a brochure describing the farm and its history.[42]

The Boys Club had begun operating a day camp even before the departure of the South End House, and after the settlement house ceased working with the farm, the Boys Club expanded its day camp, with two-week sessions that included one overnight each week. These were great days at Winning Farm, according to Edward Gaiero. As one of two drivers for the Boys Club, he took a bus full of boys to the farm, helped with activities during the day and then drove the campers back to the Boys Club for a dip in the pool in the late afternoon. Woburn resident Sue Ellen Holland, who worked at the Boys Club at the time, remembers the boys racing into the Club at the end of a hot summer day's activities and plunging gleefully into the cooling waters of the Club's swimming pool.

Ed Gaiero had taught high school biology and earth sciences for 38 years, and like the early experts in plants and animals hired by the South End House to teach children about nature, he was well equipped to

What is that thing? 1978, Don Young. Woburn Daily Times. *Winning Home Archives*

mentor the campers. On one memorable excursion to Plum Island the boys came across a dead sand shark as they made their way to the beach, and in a spontaneous biology lesson, Gaiero took out his penknife and dissected the animal, explaining its various internal systems to the boys.

At the camp there were hikes through the woods down to the Frog Pond at the easterly end of the camp, where there would be discussion of pollution and ecology, along with arts and crafts upstairs in the barn, time spent on the camp's beloved merry-go-round (affectionately referred to as "the puke-machine"), and lots of fresh air. There were also outings to Red Sox games (when you could sit in the bleachers for 50 cents, says Gaiero), Newburyport, Canobie Lake amusement park in New Hampshire, and historic sites like Minute Man Park in Concord.[43]

1974
Woburn Kiwanis Club moves a building to the farm for a new cabin.

Counselors help with the big words, August 3, 1978. Don Young. Woburn Daily Times. *Winning Home Archives*

Woburn native Scott Tully remembered the fun of going to the day camp as a young boy in the 1970s. "We would walk to the Boys Club with our lunch and a bathing suit and get on an old school bus," he recalled. "At the farm we'd split into smaller groups with individual counselors, and head for the archery range or the BB-gun range or the Frog Pond or the baseball diamond." The campers enjoyed arts and crafts, science-related projects, and activities like the then-popular tie-dyeing, a craft that originated in the protest art of the 1960s. "The counselors kept you moving!" he remembers. Then it was back to the Boys Club and the pool or gym for another couple of hours. [44]

The Boys Club did not operate a full-time overnight camp, but half of the boys—as many as 50—who ranged in age from 7 to 13, would stay the night each Thursday of a two-week day-camping session. That

night became a high point of the camping experience. As the sun went down, the boys perched on logs around a campfire and listened to ghost stories and tales of a bloodthirsty monster who inhabited the Winning Farm woods. "Wolfman" was sometimes involved. Woburn native Mark LoPresti was among the younger boys who spent the night. He was a bit nervous about "being away from home and Mom" but said he "grew up a little" as a result. [45] Getting to sleep in open-air cabins with the night sounds of the woods in their ears was likely a challenge for a lot of the boys, but the morning would bring reassuring stacks of pancakes for breakfast.

At this point in its history, Winning Farm was again serving boys, but the Boys Club also provided camping for girls, at a separate location. During the 1970s, the day camp drew as many as 800 boys per summer, marking this period as one of Winning Farm's most active. In addition, on weekends and evenings in the warm weather and through the winter months, the farm was thronged with groups using the premises for meetings, retreats, celebrations and more. Winning Home's yellowing files bulge with letters thanking the farm for hosting events, and local people still remember field days, pony rides and barbecues with hot dogs and games and spins on the merry-go-round at farm events. Joe Brown, a photographer for the *Woburn Daily Times* and other papers, recalls attending band camp in the 1970s or '80s at the farm. For a week in the summer, he said, an entire marching band trained there every day. [46]

A story in the *Woburn Daily Times* dated June 7, 1974, describes a typical event, the St. Charles Family Picnic Sunday, when first-grade students and their parents spent a day at the farm with "relay races, soft ball, dancing contests, and a scavenger hunt." The site "provided swings, slides, seesaws, a basketball area and a wading pool for small children," noted the paper. And there were also marked trails "for families who would like to take a hike in the woods." Dozens if not hundreds of similar gatherings enlivened this era at the farm. "My dad was Scout leader for Troop 500," says Roseann Lilly, whose family lived just across the street. "My mom was Girl Scout leader and we had many activities at the farm beyond just running up there to play and explore."[47] Woburn native Margaret Pinkham remembered three-legged races and riding the merry-go-round from events at the farm as a ten-year-old. "The kids would run around playing. It was like having the whole woods to yourself," she said. [48]

Winning Farm's attractive facilities along with a location that was actually nearby but seemed worlds away brought many groups in search of a place to meet or celebrate. Winning Farm provided its facilities free of charge, requesting only that groups leave the premises in good order. In the course of a few years the farm was used by the C.Y.O. of St. Barbara's Parish, the Easter Seal Society, the Boys Club of Waltham, the Greek Orthodox Church, the Boy Scouts of Winchester, the Woburn Brownies, the Melrose Camp Fire Girls, the 9th grade Confirmation class from the Hancock United Church of Christ in Lexington, the Minuteman Council of the Boy Scouts, the Walpole Camp Fire Girls, the Welcome Wagon Newcomers Club of Lexington, the Woburn 4-H Club, the Woburn Company National Guard, the Brotherhood of Temple Isaiah in Lexington, and many more, including a service-oriented fraternity from Suffolk University that agreed to paint the cottage they stayed in, and Boy Scouts who came during the winter to attain their Deep Freeze badges.

Many activities in those years revolved around horses, and Albert (Allie) Wall, former director of public works in Woburn and a caretaker at the farm for many years, oversaw countless events with pony rides for children. Many organizations that served young people with disabilities made use of the farm. "The joy on the faces of those...

youngsters who were able to ride the ponies and enjoy the grounds was a sight to behold," wrote the supervisor of special needs of the Northeast Metropolitan Region following a visit to the farm in the summer of 1975. "The parents thank you, the staff thanks you, but most of all our young people thank you," wrote the administrator of Communitas Inc. after a day of activities at the farm.

The success of this work influenced an expansion in Winning Home's mission to include children with disabilities. In 1988, Winning Home's articles of organization were amended to focus on providing services and support to children, and the families of children, who are "economically, socially, physically, emotionally or mentally handicapped or disadvantaged." The newly defined mission made it possible for Winning Home to provide support to other organizations in the form of grants.

The 1970s represented a heyday at the farm, with as much activity as any time in its history. But increasingly stringent health, safety and staffing regulations by the state began to weigh heavily on the farm's budget, especially when added to the maintenance costs of the farmhouse, now more than 150 years old, and of other structures on the site. In addition, the farm was supporting two caretakers for year-round protection against vandalism and arson (after a fire damaged one of the cabins). Indeed, financial constraints were afflicting general interest summer camps nationwide, and many closed in this period. In the 1980s, when new and unexpected costs were added to old ones, the camping days at Winning Farm would come to an end.

1988
Winning Home includes children with disabilities as part of its mission.

CHAPTER FIVE

The Old Farm in a New Era:
Leveling the playing field, unintended consequences, a re-invented organization

In response to the rising costs of operating a summer camp for children, the farm took a step toward the end of the 1970s that was to prove deeply problematic. It involved signing an option in 1979 to sell 45 acres of the farm to Choate-Symmes Hospital. Selling land in times of financial need was not an entirely new idea for Winning Home. In the 1920s, following a review of its finances, Winning Home had sold a slightly larger parcel, of 46.5 acres, to raise money.[49] Now Choate-Symmes made an offer to which Winning Home agreed, at least initially, and papers were signed.

However, the hospital did not immediately move ahead with the purchase. In fact, it did not exercise its option to buy until 1982, at which time the validity of the option depended on whether Winning Home had extended it past the original three-year deadline. On this question a dispute arose between the hospital and the farm as to whether the signer of the extension was authorized by Winning Home to do so, and whether he was physically well enough following a heart attack to assume the responsibility of formalizing

WINNING FARM FIRE - Firefighters from Woburn and Lexington aim water at flames from the old farmhouse at Winning Farm, Friday afternoon. The blaze, which is of suspicious origin, destroyed the two-story wooden structure and an adjacent barn. Crews from Woburn, Lexington, Burlington and Winchester were summoned to the scene. (Joe Brown photo.)

the agreement. The issue became a lawsuit, the first in the farm's history, that worked its way through court for several costly years. In 1987 Winning Home prevailed—in something of a pyrrhic victory. The property remained intact, but the suit devastated the farm's finances, which were already strained by another and even more unfortunate decision made by the farm around the same time in the late 1970s.

It seemed innocent enough. The topography of the farm—with its long slopes, small hills and sudden drops—had created irresistible places for kids to explore, but also made it difficult to stage games like football or baseball. Friends and associates of the farm were asked to help create a level playing field on a sloping area down the way from the main house. In the tradition of Winning Home, the arrangements were notably informal—a way of doing business that was a source of pride to the farm and its leaders, who tended toward a "can-do" approach to work projects. A call would go out to a network of supporters and soon the job was done, without anyone ever signing a contract or sending a bill for materials or services. Volunteers had rolled up their sleeves to build cabins for

Opposite: Enjoying a walk in the old Winning Farm woods, now open space, 2023. Photo by the author.

Winning Farm in the 1950s; local businesses with the know-how and equipment had transported a building to the farm to replace a structure that had burned; a nearby vocational school built a dozen new picnic tables when they were needed; a Boston college fraternity made repairs and improvements; and over the years hundreds of volunteers had offered their assistance with projects. Now, local trucking companies, one after another, would help level a few acres of the farm's hilly terrain by bringing in loads of fill. It was a case of the community helping the farm, as the farm had helped numerous community organizations by hosting their meetings, field days, retreats, annual events and more over the years—free of charge.

From the start, however, the effort encountered problems. Neighbors disliked the coming and going of the heavy trucks that rumbled past their homes taking loads of unknown material up the curving road to the farm. It was feared that the fill might contain contaminated substances that would pose a danger to the area's drinking water or cause other as yet unidentified problems. Such concerns proliferated as the trucks rolled into the farm, each load putting further strain on the cordial relations of many decades.

At that time in Woburn, a new awareness was building of the dangers of seemingly innocuous gestures like using construction and demolition materials to level a few acres of land for a ball field. People worried about what might leach out of those materials, and what long-term damage they might do to the environment, to their properties, and to the value of their homes. On the other side of town, in 1979, the same year Winning Home began bringing in fill for its ball field, authorities discovered that barrels with industrial fluid containing trichloroethylene (TCE) and perchloroethylene (PCE) had been leaking into the Aberjona River. Tests confirmed high concentrations of both organic compounds in two public drinking wells. The families of children

diagnosed with leukemia in that area subsequently filed a suit against the W. R. Grace and Beatrice Foods companies for the dumping of materials that indeed proved to be toxic.

Requests to Winning Home for documents describing its filling operation went unmet, as no such documents apparently existed. The farm ceased bringing in the fill for a time but then resumed it. Soon a neighborhood organization formed, and Winning Home found itself back in court. Neighbors insisted that the fill came from another W.R. Grace site, this one in Cambridge near the new Alewife MBTA Station.

Over the next several years, through successive rounds of soil testing by the city, the state, and eventually the federal government, no link could be found to the material from the Alewife location, and nothing was discovered in the soil at Winning Farm that represented a danger to public health or the environment. An Environmental Protection Agency report stated in 1999, "Based on the testing conducted by the Environmental Protection Agency and the review of other data collected to date at the site, the conditions at the Winning Farm landfill do not, in the Agency for Toxic Substances and Disease Registry's and our opinion pose a public health or environmental threat." [50]

Nevertheless, there were materials from demolition projects that could not be deposited legally in the ground outside of an officially designated landfill. Demolition waste, if not hazardous, was regarded as "refuse," and could be dumped only in a site officially assigned by the local Board of Health. In 1985 Winning Home reached a low point in its long history and agreed to apply for the designation of part of its property as a landfill.

After extensive litigation, a clean-up plan that would include years of continuous testing and monitoring was developed at an estimated cost of "$110,000 to $150,000 per acre," or up to $1.1 million total, according to the *Woburn Advocate*. The sum was well beyond the financial capacity of the organization, and Winning Home was faced with bankruptcy. The farm, after almost a century of service to children, was about to go under. [51]

The board of directors considered a variety of solutions to the crisis including selling the property to a well-established nonprofit organization with children's programming such as the Greater Boston YMCA. Winning Home negotiated at length with that organization and others, but the existence of the landfill complicated every effort. Some board members urged giving the land to Woburn's Conservation Commission in exchange for the city's assumption of current debts and the costs of the clean-up. But this option, even if accepted by the city, would generate no funds with which the organization could carry on its obligations under William Winning's will—as it was legally required to do.

Finances now reached a critical stage; legal bills continued to mount; soil testing costs were forcing the sale of the organization's assets; the fire and liability insurances had been cancelled for nonpayment; and, as time went by without programming for children, the IRS was threatening to rescind the farm's nonprofit status. Without that status, the farm would confront taxation of its property, and with no means of paying, would lose the land to foreclosure. After several difficult discussions among board members, it appeared that the only way to keep faith with the provisions of the Winning legacy was to part with the land and use the proceeds to help children in some new way. Fortunately, Mr. Winning had stipulated in his will that the trustees could sell the property as one way to carry out his purposes for children. Confronted with limited choices, the board held two lengthy meetings in mid-October of 1995, in the dining room of the old farmhouse, and made the hard decision to sell the farm.

Open space amenities at the old Winning Farm. Photo by the author.

A request for proposals was put together and sent out and by mid-December the board was listening to presentations from four potential purchasers. In January 1996 the board signed a purchase-and-sale agreement with Ruping and Murray, a Burlington real estate developer that agreed to a six-month window for the city of Woburn and the towns of Winchester and Lexington to decide whether to purchase the land themselves.

October 1995
Winning Home makes the painful decision to sell the farm.

A wildflower meadow in the open space at the old Winning Farm. Photo by the author.

"The children of Woburn and their families would retain access to the area, and the city would see to its preservation. More important, the funds received from the sale would make it possible for Winning Home to continue its mission of service to children—in some new form."

condominium complex off Thornberry Road in Winchester, for residents 55 and over.

Lexington passed on the chance to buy the nine acres of land within its borders, and the Lexington land was subsequently purchased from Winning Home by Ruping and Murray for $320,000 to be developed as four to six single-family house lots. [52]

And Woburn? The city considered purchasing the 60 acres of the old farm within its boundaries, but the estimated cost of $1 million to close the landfill and of $4 million to match the real estate developer proved too much for the city, especially in light of an ongoing budget crisis. Instead, the city worked out a compromise with Winning Home in an arrangement that was gaining popularity elsewhere. The city would alter the zoning restrictions to permit a developer to build clusters of townhouses if these clusters occupied just half of the land in question, while the other half went to the city as open space. As for the landfill issue, no part of the open space overlapped the landfill area, and further, the clean-up, whatever the cost, according to the *Woburn Advocate*, "would be left to the responsibility of the developer." [53]

The arrangement had clear advantages for the city of Woburn. Not only would the city acquire 30 acres of open space at no cost, it would reap

Winchester seized the opportunity and purchased the 44 acres of Winning Farm within its borders for $1.2 million—which was less than the $1.7 million the farm was asking, but more than the recent appraisal of $990,000. Excluded from the sale was approximately one acre, which was in Winchester but fell within the landfill area. (After the clean-up, Winchester paid a token $1 for ownership of this parcel.) With land values rising, the town subsequently sold 12.5 of the 44 acres to a development company for more than enough to recoup its purchase price and thus acquired 31.5 acres of open space for the town at no cost. Eventually the 12.5 acres were developed as townhouses and became Winning Farm of Winchester, which is a 29-unit an annual financial benefit. Townhouse clusters provide many services to their residents that are normally supplied by local government. "Because of reduced stress on city services...," noted a newspaper story in 1996, "the townhouses at Winning Farm would net a $300,000 positive yearly cash flow for the city, as opposed to a $100,000 net deficit if single family homes are built in the area." [54]

The compromise also appealed to Winning Home. The old farm would not be completely lost but would survive—half of it—as open space, with the pristine character of the land in the time of William Henry Winning. The children of Woburn and their families would retain access to the area, and the city would see to its preservation. More important, the funds received from the sale would make it possible for Winning Home to continue its mission of service to children—in some new form.

With this agreement in 1996 it would seem that the way was cleared for the sale to be finalized and the subsequent development to proceed. Ruping and Murray agreed to pay $4 million for the 60 acres in Woburn and build 147 townhouses while deeding half of the property to the city for open space. But in 1996, a decade of dissension still lay ahead. However appealing to the city of Woburn and Winning Home, the plan was not acceptable to all parties involved. At dozens of points in the period between the farm's decision to sell in 1995, and the granting of the final permit to build in 2006, a group of neighbors resisted the development with a succession of demands for soil testing, followed by questioning of the results, followed in turn by appeals to higher authorities, followed again by rejections of the result of the appeals and, often, by questions about the integrity, competence or scientific knowledge of the agencies or individuals involved in the process. Concerns about a "cancer cluster" in the neighborhoods around the farm dominated the headlines at one point, but studies by the state office of Health and Human Services found no "atypical

pattern" of cancer "in this area of Woburn," and noted that "many of the cancer types diagnosed and reported among the residents are not associated with environmental risk factors." [55]

Ten years of headlines in the local papers chronicled the neighbors' demands and appeals. Their concerns, whatever the particulars, appear to have centered around the fear of land and water contamination that was very much a reality in Woburn at the time. The W.R. Grace case of the 1980s came to a devastating conclusion in 1987 when the Fortune 500 company was held responsible for poisoning the community's drinking water and causing the deaths of several children. Recounted in the Hollywood movie "A Civil Action" in the late 1990s, the case had generated a new awareness of the dangers of toxic substances being dumped onto the land and into the water—a practice prevalent in Woburn throughout its history. In the 17th century, some of the nation's first tanneries were constructed along Woburn's Aberjona River, and Woburn became a major center for leather goods production into the Civil War era and beyond. The tanning of animal hides to produce leather required processes and chemicals later known to be dangerous to human health. The true impact of centuries-old practices was being felt at this moment in history, and anger, resistance, and distrust were in the air.

The sale of Winning Farm took place against this alarming background, and the difficulties were likely exacerbated by a number of other realities playing out at the time, including the rapid loss of farmland. Woburn, despite its industrial history, was largely an agricultural place, and William Winning's old homestead, surrounded by acres of fields, pastures, meadows and woodland was typical of the area well into the 20th century, when much of the population of America still lived on family farms. But change came rapidly. Between the 1940s and the 1980s, the number of farms in the nation declined precipitously.

1987
W.R. Grace found guilty of poisoning Woburn's drinking water. Massive environmental clean-up took decades.

Whereas 40 percent of the population had lived on farms in 1900, only 1 percent lived on farms in 2000.[56]

In Woburn, old farms were disappearing and new housing springing up—single family homes, clusters of houses, and even townhouses. The new homes were competitive with Boston prices and only ten miles from the city, with good auto and rail connections. They held a great appeal for buyers. But what many long-term residents saw, especially in the western part of town, where Woburn met Winchester and Lexington, was the familiar fields and pastures of their childhood simply vanishing, as farm after farm went to developers for housing. And with the fading of the farms as physical places went a certain loss of cultural significance, given the history and values of farms in American life.

As such historical forces altered the character of Woburn, the struggle over Winning Farm assumed all the more poignance in that, compared to the contest between a small group of Woburn residents and the corporate giant on the other side of town, the tug-of-war between Winning Farm and its neighbors was between one group of people concerned about the effects of potential pollution and another group of people concerned about helping children in need. The decision to sell the land carved deep divisions between the farm and its neighbors, who had had unrestricted access to the farm's hundred-plus acres of pristine landscape for as long as they could remember, and who were looking at a loss of a much-loved amenity. Local kids used Winning Farm as their backyard—one life-long neighbor said her young brother knew every inch of the farm and spent his happiest hours there looking for salamanders.[57] The farm had always been part of the local scene, and now it was about to go for housing development.

And so the soil testing and appeals of the results continued until, in 2002, after more testing, appeals and reviews, and numerous questions about the adequacy of the proposed clean-up, the Department of Environmental Protection accepted a remediation plan from the developer for the seven acres of land in question. As a front-page story in the *Daily Times Chronicle* stated on July 12 of that year, "The state Department of Environmental Protection last Friday issued its final approval for cleaning up the landfill at Winning Farm, one of three hurdles that must be cleared before townhouses can be built at the site."

A few months later, on December 18, 2002, the *Daily Times Chronicle* reported that the city council had granted the permit for 147 townhouses on the Woburn site.

Then, on February 18, 2005, almost ten years after the decision to sell, the Winning Farm project received its final permit, a determination that the development "will not result in adverse impacts to wetland resource areas," from the state Department of Environmental Protection.[58]

A year later, on February 7, 2006, the papers reported that the sale had closed and Winning Home was to receive $5 million in proceeds. Contingencies written into the purchase and sale agreement had tracked the increasing value of the land during the permitting process.

Several more years were to pass before the first structures appeared, as the developer worked through a lengthy clean-up during which he found trace amounts of asbestos from asphalt roofing shingles, which helped push the cost of remediation above $3 million. In time, the Village at Winning Farm took shape around the area where the farmhouse had been, and the transformation of a 19th century farm to a 21st century residential community was complete.

The old farm became home to two separate townhouse communities, one on the Winchester property and one on the Woburn property,

2006
Final permits for development with half of the land designated as open space.

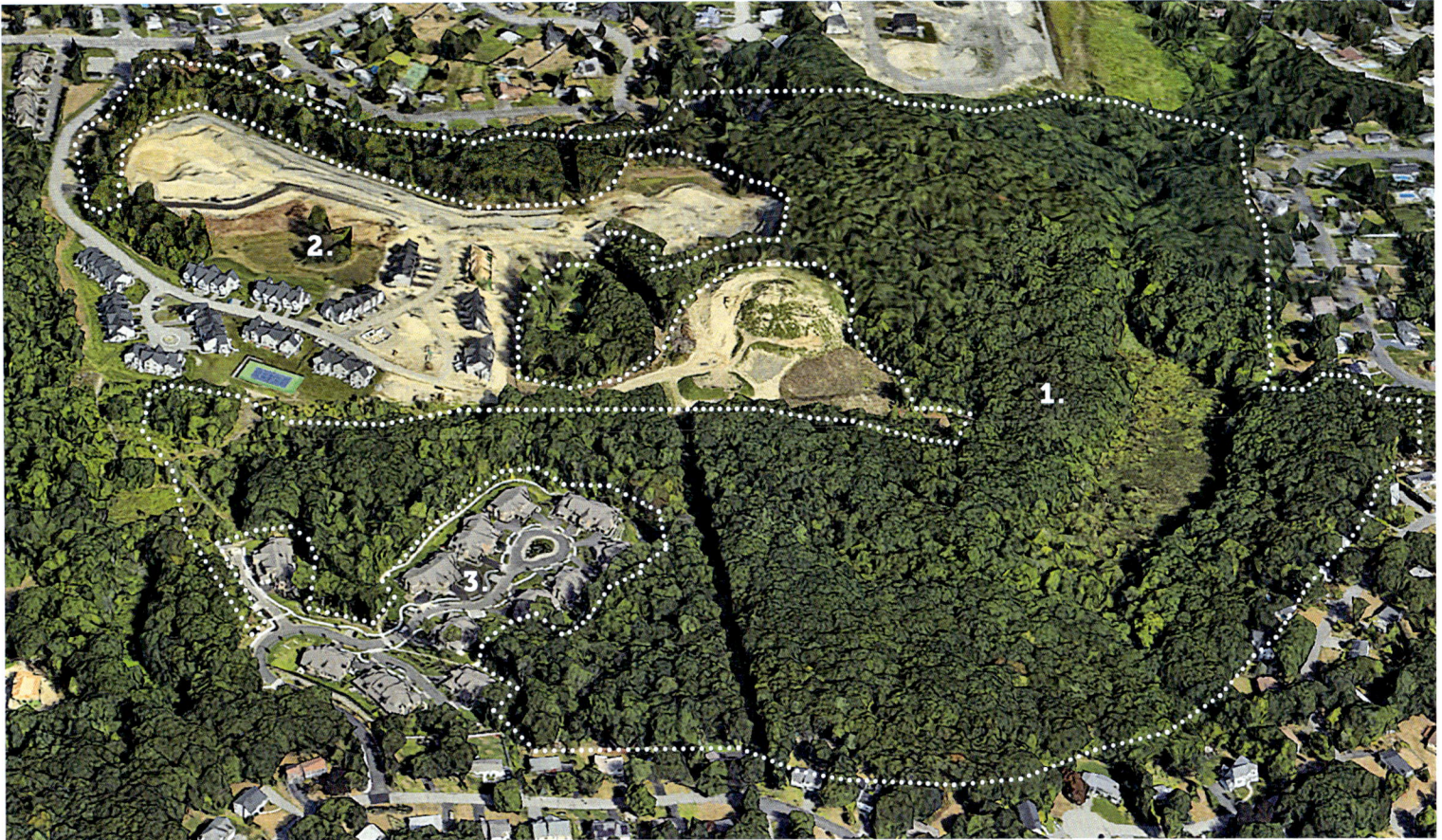

A rough outline of Winning Farm in the 21st century reveals approximately 62 acres of open space (1) as well as housing developments in Woburn (2) and Winchester (3). Retrieved from Earth.Google.com

along with a small single-family-home development in Lexington. The farm also yielded approximately 62 acres of open space, 30 acres in Woburn, which abutted 32 acres in Winchester, making up an area more than half the size of the farm when Winning Home decided to sell. This open space belongs to the people of Woburn and Winchester, in perpetuity.

In the year 2000, during the period of soil testing and legal proceedings, a massive fire destroyed the old farmhouse. During a single night the house in which William Henry Winning was born and died, went up in smoke and flames. It was the end of Mr. Winning's place, after

close to one century as a family farm, and another as a summer camp for children. But it was not the end of the benefits for children that his legacy had established.

Through the contentious period following the sale of the property, Winning Home continued to fulfill its benefactor's wishes to care for children in need. Despite a lingering nostalgia for the big house and the children singing around campfires at nightfall, the new incarnation of Winning Home prospered as the old one rarely had, reaching out to communities for miles around and helping many more children than ever in the past.

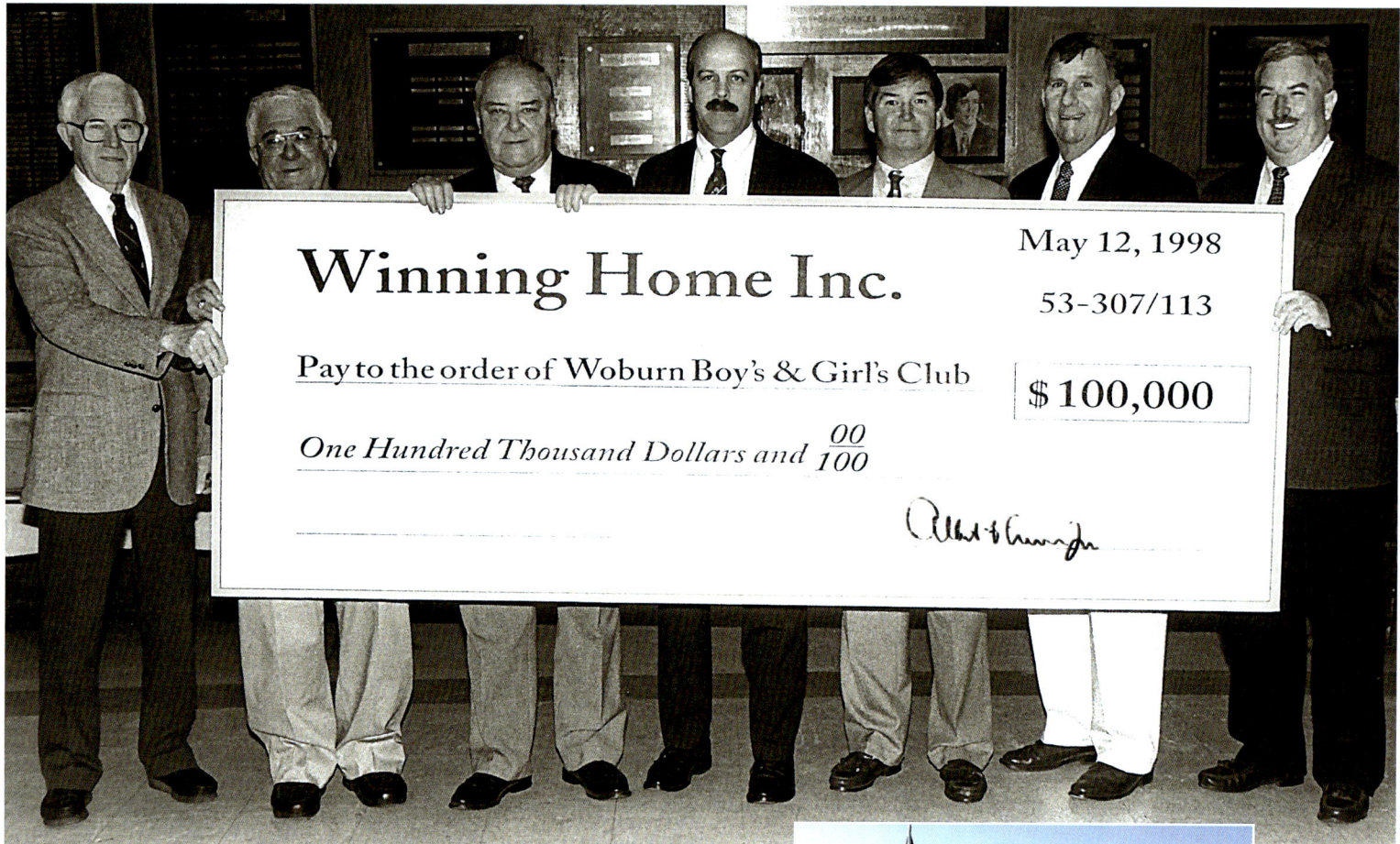

> "As soon as we became a grant maker, we realized the true potential of the Winning legacy. We quickly saw that we could help many more children than we had before."

Presenting the big check. From left, Winning Home board members Walter Farrell Jr., Harry Boodakian and Donald Foley with President Glenn Johnson of the Woburn Boys and Girls Club and Winning Home board members Albert (Chip) Curran Jr., Thomas Martin III, and Larry Byron. Winning Home Archives

Keeping the Commitment to Children:
Winning Home reinvents itself with new, varied and surprising ways to support young people

Back in the 1970s, when things were booming at the farm with a lively day camp and dozens of organizations holding events on the premises year round, Winning Home did something completely new. It established two funds of $4,000 each at the Northeast Metropolitan Regional Vocational School District in nearby Wakefield to provide two scholarships a year—one to a graduate from Woburn and one to a graduate from Winchester. Soon afterward, Winning Home established a similar fund with $4,000 at Minuteman Regional Vocational School in Lexington, for a graduate from that city. "The scholarship funds represent a new activity for the organization while reinforcing its original purpose, namely, helping youngsters," noted the *Woburn Daily Times*.

The scholarships were a genuine departure for Winning Home. Always tightly focused on the farm and activities there, Winning Home looked beyond the farm's borders for the first time and made a contribution to another organization.

Fulfilling its mission apart from the farm was a small and isolated gesture in 1977, but it suggested other ways to carry out the purposes of William Winning's bequest. In the 1990s, after the decision to sell the property, giving grants and thus investing in other organizations devoted to children became the principal function of the organization.

For so long land-rich and cash-poor, Winning Home had now become all cash. Operating with minimal overhead out of donated office space, it now had the opportunity to spend virtually all of its income across a broad spectrum of programs for children and to place every dollar where it was most needed at the time. And the dollars began mounting up as payments from the land sales began coming in.

The transformation brought a new level of energy and creativity, as well as a burst of enthusiasm, to the old organization. In 1998 Winning Home proudly made its first grant—a bold and generous $100,000—to the Woburn Boys and Girls Club, its partner in bringing children to the farm in the 1970s and '80s. Now Winning Home offered funds to help build an expanded clubhouse and support dozens of new programs.

And that was just the start. According to long-time board treasurer Albert (Chip) Curran Jr., whose office housed the organization, "As soon as we became a grant maker, we realized the true potential of the Winning legacy. We quickly saw that we could help many more children than we had before. Yes, it was a wrenching transition, but we very soon realized that we gained much more than we had lost." Commented Thomas Martin III, who had been a member of the farm's board since 1968, "In terms of what we could do for children, I can only say that it

MAY 1998
Winning Home makes its first grant.

was a great new day for Winning Home." Images of board members handing six-foot-long checks to organizations began to appear in the papers, with broad smiles all around.

Throughout its first century, Winning Home's assistance to children had been very direct, as the organization worked first with nonprofits in Boston to bring children to the Woburn farm for fresh-air vacations and camping and then focused on local children through the day camp established by the Woburn Boys Club. Now Winning Home evolved from a place of refuge to a source of funds reaching children across the three communities the farm overlapped—Woburn, Winchester and Lexington—and well into surrounding cities and towns, with grants going to organizations in Reading, Arlington, Concord, Gloucester, Lynn, Lowell and beyond.

In its new role as grantmaker, Winning Home broadened its reach into young lives, supplying funds to 15 to 20 organizations every year that provide families with food and shelter through pantries and daycare, help unhoused children get housed again through gifts of furniture to their families, offer free day care for young kids so their parents can work, fund a place to go before and after school to meet with friends and learn new things, offer training in the arts to help young people develop the healthy and powerful identities that are often damaged by poverty, provide assistance to children with disabilities through equestrian therapy, and reach out to kids struggling with the loss of a parent—that is, helping with everything from very basic physical needs to the therapeutic, creative, emotional, even existential needs of children. In its second century of helping children Winning Home remains a modest operation, with a single paid employee and a financial consultant, but its reach is very broad and very deep. "Big enough to be helpful, small enough to be personal," as one grantee described Winning Home.

In its new incarnation Winning Home found dozens of vital uses for the funds it now had available to share. What organizations did it choose to fund? What were they like? If one were to tour just a few of Winning Home's grantees on an ordinary day in the third decade of the 21st century, one might encounter the following scenes:

At the **Woburn Boys and Girls Club**, Winning Home's original grantee, some kids are swimming in the big pool, others are playing basketball in the gym, doing homework with friends in a quiet room with comfortable chairs, grabbing a treat in the snack-bar run as a business by club members, building bed frames in a community service project, or learning how to do computer coding—enjoying themselves in a safe, friendly, educational place before and after school, while their parents are off at work, confident that their children are safe and cared for. **Following its first gift in 1998 Winning Home has become one of the Club's largest private donors, giving a total of $1,840,000 by 2023.**

A big check arrives at a long-time grantee. Council of Social Concern, Woburn, Massachusetts.

Making friends with the resident guinea pig. Council of Social Concern, Woburn, Massachusetts.

At the **Council of Social Concern in Woburn**, young children are taking their afternoon naps on low-slung beds in dim classrooms while their teachers watch over them—and their parents are at work. The day care is free for many families (at a time when private child care in Massachusetts averages $3,000 a month), and the feeling is warm and welcoming, with a pet lizard and a much-loved guinea pig in residence. Down the hall from the napping children, a volunteer is stacking bottles of juice on a shelf in the small food pantry for neighbors who will arrive soon for a box of food. At the same time, a client is applying to the emergency fund for the $50 that might be needed to avoid eviction or for a small sum to keep the electricity on.

A long-term funder, Winning Home was the Council's key donor when it expanded to its new facility. Between 2001 and 2023, Winning Home provided the organization with $1,703,500 in grants.

In Reading, at the **Mission of Deeds**, you walk into a sprawling high-ceilinged warehouse through mazes of goods: rolled-up blankets and kitchen wares (pots and pans and tea kettles); back-to-back sofas in long rows; a small room full of table lamps and standing lamps; a long shelf of children's books with glossy covers; dozens of children's puffy winter coats bulging from a long rack; desks large and small; and an extensive collection of bureaus—all awaiting distribution to people emerging from homelessness and others in need. Keep going and you come to a small workshop where volunteers are repairing and updating old furniture for new owners. The sum total is a museum-scale collection of objects needed for living, being transferred from

A warehouse of furniture helps families start new homes. Mission of Deeds, Reading, Massachusetts

donors to recipients by way of an organization skilled in this special human-to-human exchange. Adding to the place's unique atmosphere is a number of skillfully designed stained-glass windows, the artwork of the founder's son. He remains part of the operation, in homage to his father, the owner of a successful auto-parts business who launched the organization in 1993.

"Our first client was a woman who kept her children's clothes in trash bags," says an administrator. "We were able to give her two bureaus." He cites another client who said, "My son is 11 years old and this is his first bed." In its brief three decades, the Mission of Deeds has furnished apartments for 15,000 families.

Between 2001 and 2022 Winning Home awarded this organization grants totaling $170,000.

Walk into the old building housing **RAW Art Works** in downtown Lynn and you find yourself in a big gallery with a wall 40 or 50 feet long sporting a line of white high-top sneakers, each painted with an image that tells a story. You're experiencing just one of hundreds of creative projects going on in this place, where kids come to learn how to make art as a from of self-expression and self-validation. Like the shoes, the art made here says who I am and where I'm going, and says it with a remarkable exuberance that can be felt in the air.

The place is a bonanza of creative possibilities: four floors with walls covered in life-size images of local kids and lined with shelves of tools and materials for making things. In the basement is what looks like an old printing press with movable type; upstairs on one floor is a video studio; one end of another floor is taken up with a table six times the size of an ordinary dining table for assembling large-scale projects out of paper or fabric or paints or markers. There's a young person at the table now, bent over a small notebook and furiously writing a story, despite

RAW art projects frame the artists and spill out onto the sidewalk. Raw Art Works, Lynn, Massachusetts.

the hubbub around her, with a dozen kids talking and laughing and going at their own projects.

RAW Art is an art-teaching space but even more it's a place for kids to tell their stories, to be seen and heard. In one of the four studios is a group of kids talking about a film they're cooking up. In an example of their work on the organization's website an elderly Cambodian woman tells how she was forced out of her home by the Khmer Rouge. The filmmaker is the woman's great-granddaughter.

Since its founding in 1994 RAW Art, says its website, has been about "igniting the desire to create and fueling the confidence to succeed." Winning Home, from 2006 to 2023, provided $255,000 to support these aims.

> *"I asked myself who is lost when someone dies. It is more than simply a life that is lost. We also lose a relationship, the self we were in that relationship and a way of life in which the deceased played a role."*
>
> — Phyllis Silverman, Co-founder

When you go to **The Children's Room**, you find not just a room but an entire three-story house on a residential street, where rooms are painted deep blue or cinnamon brown, and comfortably furnished with sofas and easy chairs and soft rugs on the floor. There are no hard edges here—it is the opposite of institutional. But some serious and intense encounters are happening in these attractive spaces every day. Children who have lost a parent or sibling are getting help here—from other children who have lost a parent or sister or brother, too.

In Massachusetts one in 14 people will experience the loss of a family member by the time they are 18, and there's not a lot of help for grief in a society uncomfortable with death and not always good at talking about it. The Children's Room, which started as a single room in a hospice, does not encourage children to forget the parent who is gone, or to "get over" their loss, but instead to honor and commemorate the person who has died. Through the creative use of art, music, play and poetry, kids tend to open up and share their stories, talking or writing or drawing or making objects to express what may be among the deepest feelings humans have. Some kids just listen but still discover that they are not alone.

The Children's Room now serves about 1,500 people a year, with families meeting on alternate weeks, usually over a period of one-to-three years. There is no charge. Between 2005 and 2023, Winning Home gave $130,000 in grants to this organization.

The Children's Room offers arts and social activities and more to help children cope with loss. The Children's Room, Arlington, Massachusetts.

Every year more than 2,500 volunteers help with the farm chores. Gaining Ground Farm, Concord, Massachusetts.

When you drive up the crunchy gravel road that leads to **Gaining Ground Farm** in Concord, where every vegetable grown is given to hunger-relief organizations, you see fields where groups of volunteers are helping to plant, cultivate and harvest crops. The farm hosts as many as 2,500 volunteers a season on its three acres, and many of those volunteers are young students from local schools. They are discovering how Brussels sprouts grow, or that a potato "seed" is the entire potato, or they are helping to haul a cartload of just-picked red peppers to the washing station. At the same time they are learning life lessons about community service and helping to provide food for kids their age who don't have enough to eat. Every year Gaining Ground's work with hunger-relief organizations helps to feed the thousands of children in eastern Massachusetts whose families cannot feed them adequately. **Between 2013 and 2023, Winning Home provided $126,000 to Gaining Ground, helping fund projects like digging a new well to improve irrigation and building a plastic-sheathed hoop house that can extend the growing season by more than a month.**

A final stop in this mini-tour of Winning Home's grantees could take you to **Lovelane Special Needs Horseback Riding Program** in Lincoln, where you witness a kind of therapy that is provided, remarkably, by horses. Inside the spacious and sweet-smelling barn you walk past box stalls where solemn-looking horses nibble strands of hay from the floor and lift their heads to look at you. When a horse is led past you, its thousand-pound presence and confident stride create a sensation. This is a big animal! The barn's two pet cats move quickly aside.

Entering the large, well lighted arena, you see what it is these animals can do. From a platform at one end of the space, a young child who can neither walk nor speak due to a range of medical conditions, is lifted from a wheelchair and placed on the back of a horse. You may feel nervous at this point. But aides on either side hold the rider in place and then, slowly, the horse begins to move. The horse pads slowly toward the far end of the arena, through shafts of bright sunshine coming in big windows, and makes a broad turn. And that's it, to all appearances.

But what is happening here is two things: The rhythmic motions of the horse's muscles as it walks help strengthen the muscles the child needs to sit up, which the three-year-old on its back has never been able to do. At the same time, the child and the horse are developing a relationship that is notably intimate. If the horse senses fear or anxiety in the rider, it is likely to halt in its tracks. The attendants may urge the horse onward, but it will likely refuse to move until the child is calm.

The impact of this almost invisible therapy can be profound. The counselors at the farm say that they have heard children unable to speak say their first word. Children unable to walk have taken their first steps.

Riding is an intense activity, eventually permitting some children usually confined to a wheelchair to control a thousand-pound animal. With time the rider can develop a sense of self as strong, independent

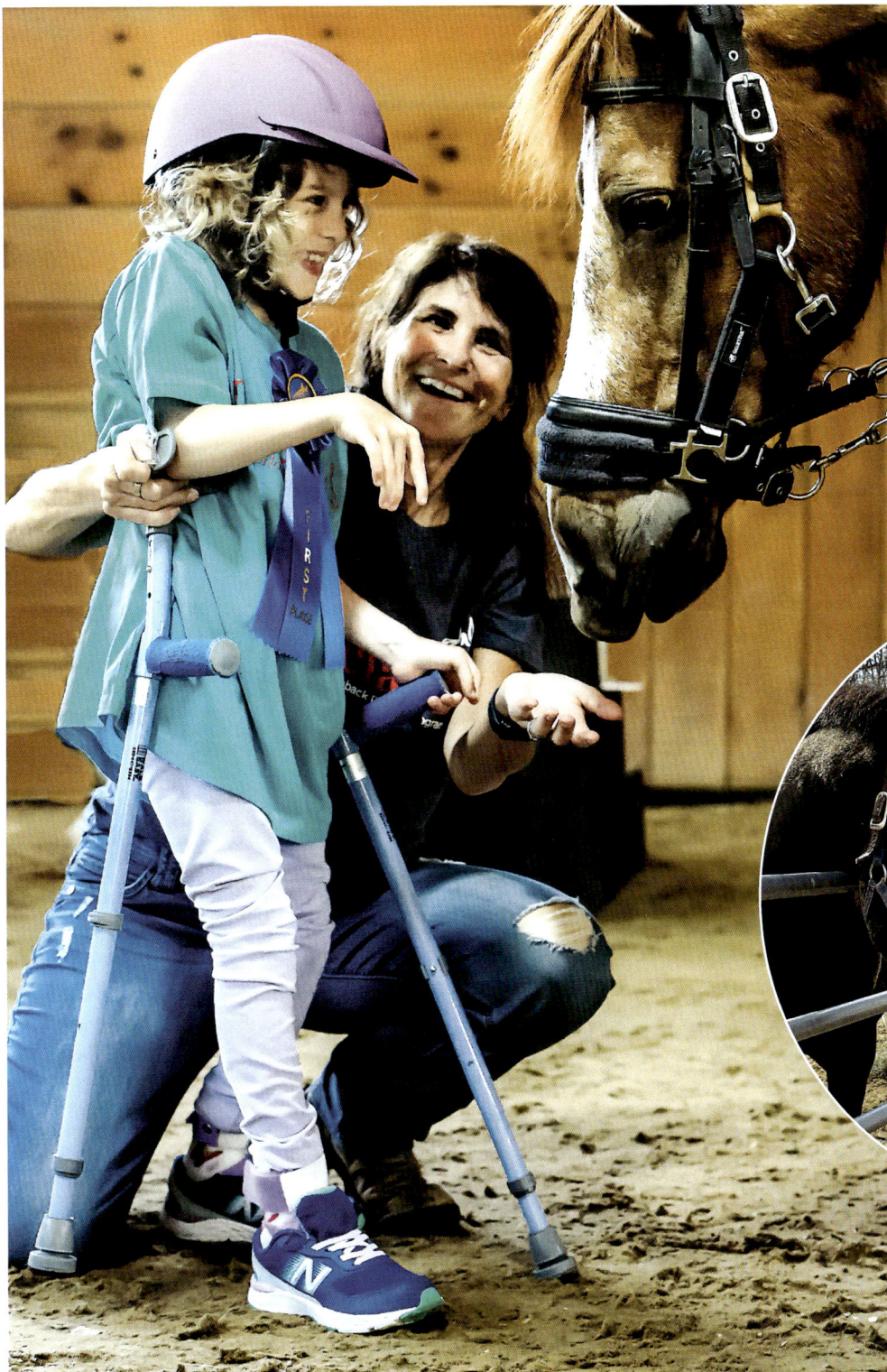

*Lovelane founder Debby Sabin introduces
a young client to the therapist.
Lovelane Special Needs Horseback
Riding Program, Lincoln, Massachusetts.*

Below, Therapists Cactus and Abe.

and athletic—an empowerment that can transfer into the rest of a person's life. On a horse, a child who normally looks up at the world from a wheelchair suddenly looks down on it. Children with the severest disabilities have a genuine opportunity to excel.

The benefits of this therapy are so striking that a second horse-therapy facility, **Strongwater Farm Therapeutic Equestrian Center** in Tewksbury, was added to the list of Winning Home's grantees. "Winning Home believed in us," said the director, as Strongwater began building a new arena in 2018, and started to expand its programs. In addition to children's therapy, Strongwater offers a program for police, fire-fighters and first responders.

This focus on horses and their connections to children may be a link to the old farm where for many years horseback riding was a favorite activity. Winning Farm's long-time caretaker Allie Wall loved horses and offered pony rides at countless birthday parties and other events for children. In addition, a local group staged horse shows on the property to give young people an opportunity to demonstrate their riding skills, while raising funds for charity. In the farm's new incarnation, some of the best times of the past are being memorialized, always with children as the beneficiaries.

Between 2011 and 2023, Winning Home made grants totaling $80,000 to Lovelane, and to the newer grantee, Strongwater Farm, between 2018 and 2023, a total of $30,000.

Winning Home is proud to contribute to these and many other organizations helping to make the lives of young people healthier, happier, easier, and just better. The plan is for Winning Home to continue to provide for children in these and ever-newer and increasingly effective ways into the future.

Afterword

Poverty in America has not been resolved in the century and more that have passed since William Winning, farmer and philanthropist, wrote out his will on a June day at his sprawling farm in Woburn, Massachusetts. Children have always been the poorest segment of our society, and neither the advances of modernity nor the wealth of a great nation have altered that fact. Even in a prosperous state like Massachusetts, many young people are homeless. Many families rely on food banks to feed their children. And across the country many young people are working in dangerous environments at an early age.

Nevertheless, countless children benefit from organizations like those the Woburn farmer's legacy supports. There's no question about that. And there's more. At the horse stable, or the food pantry, or the day care place, or the used furniture warehouse, or at the arts school in Lynn, if you are fortunate enough to take a tour like that described above, you have an opportunity to see what can only be called human goodness in action. It's valuable to observe the people in charge, and the people working in these places, and the people volunteering there. To be in their presence, as the author of this history can attest, is a profound experience.

Acknowledgements

Sincere thanks for helping create this history go to the many people who shared their memories and knowledge of Winning Home throughout its days as a farm, summer camp, community gathering place and grant-making institution. These generous individuals include Edward Gaiero, Joseph Gaiero, Scott Tully, Joe Brown, Margaret Pinkham, Roseann Lilly, Maureen Willis, Sue Ellen Holland, Mark LoPresti, Daniel Wall and Carra Wall. The author is especially grateful to long-term board members Thomas Martin III and Albert (Chip) Curran Jr.—who guided Winning Home's transition from a traditional summer camp to a 21st century grant-making institution—for their reflections on the organization's history, and with board member Robert Maguire, for their thoughtful reviews of the text. Many thanks to Dolores Pollock and Paul Johnson for detailed commentary throughout. Special thanks to Kate Canfield for her creative, appropriate and beautiful design work.

Special thanks for their descriptions and insights into the work supported by Winning Home in its role as a grant-maker go to several nonprofit organizations whose staff members graciously took the time to meet with the author, talk about the mission and history of their work, and provide tours of their facilities. Representing a small sampling of Winning Home's grantees, these individuals include: Maria Antonioni, executive director, Strongwater Farm Therapeutic Equestrian Center, Inc., Tewksbury; Jesse Bencosme, executive director, and Amanda Harvey, director of public relations and development, Council of Social Concern, Woburn; Kim Cayer, philanthropy director, The Children's Room, Arlington; Kerry Fitzgerald, grants officer, Pathways for Children, Gloucester; Julie Gage, executive director, James L. McKeown Boys and Girls Club of Woburn; Kit Jenkins, former executive director, and Rosario Ubiera-Minaya, executive director of RAW Art Works, Lynn; David McIsaac, executive director, Sharon Petersen, director of grants, Bruce Murison, warehouse manager, and Arthur Triglione, treasurer, Mission of Deeds, Reading; Julie LaFontaine, president & CEO, and Andrew Dunn, director of grants, The Open Door, Gloucester; Judy Normandin, senior grant writer, UTEC, Lowell; Debbie Sabin, founder, Wendy Bell, executive director, and Eliza Wall, development director, Lovelane Special Needs Horseback Riding Program, Lincoln; and Maureen Willis, executive director, Woburn Community Educational Foundation, Woburn.

Thanks for assistance in organizing historic materials go to Christine Collari, executive assistant to the Winning Home Board of Directors, and for locating historic photography to Ashley Serveiss and Linda Olsson at the Woburn Public Library Archives and to Ellen Knight at the Winchester Archival Center.

Sources

This history derives in large part from the official records of Winning Home, Inc., dating to the origin of the organization circa 1900, including the minutes of board meetings and the numerous files of correspondence, and from the organization's extensive collection of newspaper clippings covering more than a century. Key newspapers include the *Woburn Daily Times*, the *Daily Times Chronicle* and the *Winchester Star*. The *Boston Globe*, the *Boston Herald American*, the *Wilmington Town Crier*, and the *Boston Evening Transcript* are also represented in the collection. These records are stored at the professional offices of Albert (Chip) Curran Jr., long-time treasurer of the organization, in Concord, Massachusetts. Christine Collari, executive assistant to the Board of Directors, oversees the collection; she provided invaluable assistance in assembling and making available these and other archival materials.

A valuable source of information was Winning Home material compiled by Jack Kean, of the Rotary Club of Winchester, Massachusetts, a service organization that adopted Winning Farm as a charitable project in the 1950s. The compilation, with an introduction by Mr. Keane, is available on the Winchester Rotary Club website. It includes a copy of William Henry Winning's Last Will and Testament, an 1899 map of the farm, a brochure with a brief history of Winning Farm through 1975, the Winning Farm song (dated 1904), an article about the sale of the farm by Winchester town archivist Ellen Knight, and many newspaper clippings and photos. Among the newspaper clippings is a valuable history of Winning Home assembled by Woburn resident Susan DeTeso and the research branch of Winning Farm Volunteers, which was published in two parts in the *Daily Times Chronicle* in 1998.

Other useful sources were the website of the City of Woburn, which includes a time-line of the city's past; the Woburn Public Library, including its newspaper and photo collections and its archives; the Woburn Historical Society, with its library of videos; and the Winchester Archival Center, which includes a photo collection.

Both Ancestry.com and MyHeritage.com provided definitive dates in the Winning family history through U.S. Census data, vital records, newspaper references and other documents. Several newspaper obituaries marked the passing of William Henry Winning; the *Woburn News* of October 29, 1898, offered the single (if very brief) contemporary commentary on Winning's life.

Information about Reverend George Landor Perin, the original director of the farm's summer camping program, came from several contemporary newspaper accounts and a book, *The House that Love Built: The History of the Franklin Square House*, published circa 2009, which memorialized Perin's role in the founding and leadership of that institution. The book, by Beth Hinchliffe and Bonnie Hurd Smith, is available from the Franklin Square House Foundation, Boston, Massachusetts.

The role of the settlement house movement in Boston derived from many online articles, the website of United South End Settlements (USES), and books by Robert A. Woods, the founder of the South End House and a national leader of the movement. He worked closely with Winning Home in its early days.

Sources of historic photographs include the Woburn Public Library archives, especially the Thomas J. Glennon Collection, the Lester Fuller Smith Photograph Collection at the Winchester Archival Center, and the newspapers noted above. Additional photography was contributed by Winning Home grantees and the author.

Wrapping up Parents and Family Day at summer camp in the 1950s with a rendition (one guesses) of the Winning Farm song. Patrick J. Farino. Courtesy, Woburn Public Library, Glennon Archives

Endnotes

1. *Woburn News*, William Henry Winning obituary, October 29, 1898.

2. DeTeso, Susan, and the Research Branch of the Winning Farm Volunteers, "Winning Farm Turns 100," a compilation by Jack Kean, Winchester Rotary Club, https://www.winchesterrotary.org/sitepage/our-winchester-club-history.

3. *Boston Globe*, John Winning (brother of William Henry Winning) obituary, October 13, 1905.

4. Franchino, Elise, "Celebrating Women in Early Childhood Education," blog post, March 25, 2019, https://www.newamerica.org/education-policy/edcentral/celebrating-women-early-childhood-education/.

5. "'Must a woman…give it all up when she marries?': The Debate over Employing Married Women as Teachers," December 18, 2014, Montana Women's History, https://montanawomenshistory.org/must-a-woman-give-it-all-up-when-she-marries-the-debate-over-employing-married-women-as-teachers/.

6. DeTeso.

7. DeTeso.

8. DeTeso.

9. Bell, Michael M., "Did New England Go Downhill?" *Geographical Review*, Vol 79, No. 4 (Oct. 1989), American Geographical Society. http://www.jstor.org/stable/215118.

10. "Woburn: A Farming Community," May 2011 (video), Woburn Historical Society, https://www.woburn historicalsociety.com/-whs-videos.

11. "Child Labor 1900: Records of Rights," US National Archives and Records Administration, http://recordsofrights.rg/events/30/child-labor.

12. "Child Labor During the Industrial Revolution," Museum of Tolerance, MOT.com, Los Angeles, California, https://www.museumoftolerance.com/assets/documents/children-who-labor-handout-2.pdf.

13. Keiger, Dale, "The Rise and Demise of the American Orphanage," *Johns Hopkins Magazine*, April 1996, https://pages.jh.edu/jhumag/496web/orphange.html

14. Gershon, Livia, "Summer Camp Has Always Been About Escaping Modern Life," *JSTOR Daily*, April 26, 2016, https://daily.jstor.org/history-summer-camp/.

15. Nadel, Meryl, and Scher, Susan, *Not Just Play: Summer Camp and the Profession of Social Work*, p. 4 (New York: Oxford University Press) 2019.

16. Winning Home, "A Brief Review of the Work Done at Winning Home 1898-1918," February 4, 1918, Winning Home archives, Office of Albert Curran, Concord, Massachusetts.

17. DeTeso.

18. Hinchliffe, Beth, and Smith, Bonnie Hurd, *The House that Love Built, The History of the Franklin Square House* (Boston: Franklin Square House Foundation) ca. 2009.

19. *Winchester Star*, June 23, 1905.

20. *Boston Globe*, August 12, 1905.

21. *Boston Globe*, July 23, 1905.

22. *Boston Globe*, August 12, 1905.

23. *Boston Evening Transcript*, John Winning obituary, October 3, 1905.

24. *Boston Globe*, July 7, 1901.

25. Robert A. Woods, Letter to Trustees of Winning Farm, September 14, 1909, Winning Home archives.

26. Blum, Deborah, *The Poison Squad: One Chemist's Single-Minded Crusade for Food Safety at the Turn of the Twentieth Century*, citing Farmer, Fannie, *Food and Cookery for the Sick and Convalescent*, 1907.

27. *Boston Evening Transcript*, July 11, 1912.

28. Winning Home, ""A Brief Review of the Work Done at Winning Home 1898-1918," a/k/a "The Twenty Year Report," Winning Home Archives, February 4, 1918.

29. Nelson, Larz F., "History: Horse thief Swain had an inheritance," *Wilmington Town Crier*, November 9, 2019.

30. Winchester Rotary Club, Wheeler sale recorded in Deed book 4645, page 201.

31. Direct Cremation of Maine, obituary of Thelma Ham Hayward (1910-2014), https://directcremationofmaine.com/tribute/details/13793/Thelma-Hayward/obituary.html.

32. Winslow, Richard S., "The South End and the South End House Today and Tomorrow," South End House report, 1944.

33. "Winning Farm Happy Home to Boston Children," Woburn Daily Times, undated clipping, ca.1958.

34. Federation of South End Settlements Newsletter, South End House, September 1958.

35. Kean, Jack, Introduction, Winchester Rotary Club, Winning Farm History. https://clubrunner.blob.core.windows.net/00000010055/en-us/files/homepage/10-winning-farm-part-1/10.-Winning-Farm-Part-1.pdf.

36. *Winchester Star*, July 9, 1954.

37. Kean.

38. Rockefeller Foundation, "Suburban Poverty in the US," May 2013. https://www.rockefellerfoundation.org/wp-content/uploads/Suburban-Poverty-in-the-United-States.pdf.

39. James L. McKeown Boys and Girls Club of Woburn, https://bgcwoburn.org.

40. Brady, Patricia, personal interview with Joseph Gaiero, Facilities Manager, James L. McKeown Boys and Girls Club of Woburn, January 13, 2023.

41. *Woburn Daily Times*, June 2, 1975.

42. *Woburn Daily Times*, June 2, 1975.

43. Brady, Patricia, personal interview with Edward Gaiero, former staff member, Boys and Girls Club of Woburn, and retired high school biology teacher, September 27, 2022.

44. Brady, Patricia, personal interview with Scott Tully, Woburn resident, January 13, 2023.

45. Brady, Patricia, personal interview with Mark LoPresti, Woburn resident, October 19, 2023.

46. Brady, Patricia, telephone interview with Joe Brown, Woburn photographer, February 9, 2023.

47. Brady, Patricia, telephone conversation with Roseann Lilly, Woburn resident, December 6, 2021.

48. Brady, Patricia, telephone conversation with Margaret Pinkham, Woburn resident, December 6, 2021.

49. Kean.

50. Environmental Protection Agency, 1999, cited in Winning Home, "The Truth About Winning Home, Inc." *Daily Times Chronicle*, p. 3A, October 11, 2001.

51. Ross, Michelle, "Mayor Backs Compromise on Winning Farm Site," *Woburn Advocate*, May 23, 1996.

52. Haggerty, James, "Winning Home, Inc., sees permit delays hurting charities," *Daily Times Chronicle*, April 25, 2002.

53. Ross.

54. Haggerty, James, "Townhouse proposal on tight deadline, *Woburn Daily Times*, May 29, 1996.

55. Vincent, Gordon, "State board finds cancer incidents are 'not atypical,'" *Daily Times Chronicle*, September 7, 2001; and Fontecchio, Mark, and Gibbs, Joseph, "Winning Farm withdraws permit request—for now," *Woburn Advocate*, December 6, 2001.

56. Lusk, Jayson, "The Evolution of American Agriculture," June 27, 2016, http://jaysonlusk.com/blog/2016/6/26/the-evolution-of-american-agriculture/.

57. Brady, Patricia, telephone conversation with Maureen Willis, Woburn resident, December 5, 2022.

58. Haggerty, James, "Winning Farm project receives its final permit," *Woburn Daily Times Chronicle*, February 18, 2005.

About the Author

Patricia J. Brady writes histories, editorials and articles for nonprofit organizations in Greater Boston. She lives in Gloucester, Massachusetts.